Making a Difference in the Classroom

The Reality and Truth of Teaching in Schools Today

Charlese E. Brown

ROWMAN & LITTLEFIELD EDUCATION
A division of
ROWMAN & LITTLEFIELD PUBLISHERS, INC.
Lanham • New York • Toronto • Plymouth, UK

This book was placed by the Educational Design Services LLC literary agency

Published by Rowman & Littlefield Education
A division of Rowman & Littlefield Publishers, Inc.
A wholly owned subsidiary of The Rowman & Littlefield Publishing Group, Inc.
4501 Forbes Boulevard, Suite 200, Lanham, Maryland 20706
www.rowman.com

10 Thornbury Road, Plymouth PL6 7PP, United Kingdom

Copyright © 2012 by Charlese E. Brown

All rights reserved. No part of this book may be reproduced in any form or by any electronic or mechanical means, including information storage and retrieval systems, without written permission from the publisher, except by a reviewer who may quote passages in a review.

British Library Cataloguing in Publication Information Available

Library of Congress Cataloging-in-Publication Data
Brown, Charlese E., 1959-
  Making a difference in the classroom : the reality and truth of teaching in schools today / Charlese E. Brown.
    pages cm
  Includes index.
  ISBN 978-1-61048-551-7 (cloth : alk. paper)—ISBN 978-1-61048-552-4 (pbk. : alk. paper)—ISBN 978-1-61048-553-1 (electronic)
 1. Teaching—United States. 2. Teachers—Training of—United States. I. Title.
  LB1715.B746 2012
  371.102—dc23
                                                                                                 2012000350

∞™ The paper used in this publication meets the minimum requirements of American National Standard for Information Sciences—Permanence of Paper for Printed Library Materials, ANSI/NISO Z39.48-1992. Printed in the United States of America

This book is dedicated to God who makes all things possible; to my husband and best friend; my children, my grandchildren, my family and friends, my parents; the committed teachers who influenced me; and to the thousands of students who have taught me well throughout the years.

I am still learning!

"How happy I am to realize that I am little and weak, how happy I am to see myself so imperfect."

—Saint Theresa

"I am only one, but still I am one. I cannot do everything, but still I can do something; and because I cannot do everything, I will not refuse to do something that I can do."

—Helen Keller

Table of Contents

Acknowledgments	ix
Introduction	1

Part I: Enter Reality

1	Your New Name	11
2	Defend Yourself	17
3	Do Our Standards Promote Equality?	31
4	Who Needs Laws?	35
5	Does Certification Prepare You for the Classroom?	37

Part II: What to Expect from Classroom Teaching

6	Salary	45
7	Taxes	51
8	Your Student Loan	53
9	Gossip	55
10	Keeping Fit	59
11	Illness	61
12	It's Lunch Time	69

13	The Players' Network	73
14	Know Your Rights	75
15	Using the School Computer	77
16	It's *Your* Attitude	81

Conclusion: The New American Classroom   83

Acknowledgments

Thank God for the fortitude to stick with this project.

Thanks to my family for putting up with my seclusion while dedicating my efforts to producing a book that will help lots of people.

Thanks to my parents—my first teachers.

Thanks to the many family and friends I have in the teaching profession, who have taught me a great deal over the years.

Thank you to Educational Design Services for recognizing the niche for and timeliness of this project.

Thank you to Rowman and Littlefield for a chance at having my voice heard.

May God bless you.

Introduction

"All truths are easy to understand once they are discovered; the point is to discover them."

—Galileo Galilee

How can anyone make a difference in today's classrooms without understanding the part ethics plays in teaching effectively? Statistics regarding student achievement are certainly testifying against our present educational structure. How can this trend be reversed without losing children or teachers in the process? How can the achievement gap between minorities and whites be closed? How can we reduce the dropout rate while attracting the most gifted teachers?

By the time you complete this book, you will have a better understanding of what really goes on inside today's classrooms and what we can do to meet the educational challenges. By knowing the truth and facing the reality of what actually takes place inside of the classroom, we can have better tools available to fix the problem.

It is time that we deal with our education challenges in a head-on fashion. Enough time has elapsed in studying data and trying programs that yield little to no results. This crisis calls for drastic measures.

If we care about what our children learn, who teaches them, and how well they learn, then it becomes imperative that we have a frank discussion about the teaching profession and the entire education system as it exists today.

The information here can help you determine if you wish to pursue teaching as a career. You will be able to determine if you have what it takes to be a teacher. If you are currently in a position that influences school policy, then you may spot solutions that will help to right the heeling ship of failing schools.

Knowing as much as we know about why schools fail, we should not still be having a conversation about failing schools. Throughout the 1980s and 1990s, researchers completed enough research on students, teachers, and how schools operate to have a viable solution by now. Yet, we continue to do more research—while losing millions of students in the process.

Volumes of information have been disseminated regarding best practices for school personnel. But the problems still remain. In some instances, problems have worsened. What have we learned? When will we put what we know into practice?

The area of concern is not the data. The concern primarily deals with equality. The apparent attitude in this country is rooted in disparity. Whether we consider money for school resources or expenditures per student, we see disparity. This disparity has persisted since the inception of public schools in this country.

To distract us away from the true problem, some notable people have suggested that it must be a money problem. Let's throw money at the problem and the problem will go away. That has been done, and the dropout rate persists. So, money can't be the answer.

Some organizations jumped on the bandwagon early, thinking that it might be classroom management, and sold a ton of material to schools that bought into this notion.

The most recent line of attack focuses on teacher accountability. How can we make teachers more accountable? Yes, how can we hold teachers even more accountable for the thousands of tasks they accomplish each and every day? Some research gives credence to the theory that advanced degrees have little to no effect on student achievement.

Teaching is probably the only profession in the world in which an advanced degree is said to have no effect on results. In the corporate world, people are encouraged to seek advanced degrees. So, what is the real problem?

Don't be fooled by seeing a little progress in our educational system. The underlying problem of disparity and the acceptance of disparity as a normal part of our society are leading to the collapse of our educational structure. When will we get it?

In every school report, there is an entry for the poverty index, economically disadvantaged children, and at-risk children. For too long, we have thought that money was the root of the problem. The thinking goes: if we supply this school with more money over that school, then our problem should be resolved. Well, that has not happened.

The consequences of this kind of thinking include more enrollments in private schools, more children on the voucher system, and the rise of more charter schools. It's not the money fueling the disparity. It's the thinking.

Undoubtedly, the notion of a free and public education is slowly disappearing. The notion of public education is turning into a charter and for-profit education system. How can this country be prepared for global competition and innovation by using these structures while abandoning public schools?

Additionally, it is no secret that school districts all over the nation are taking a closer look at how students learn. Little is being done to find ways to attract gifted teachers. Of course, money is being spent on training teachers, but very minimal effort is being put into discovering how to identify people who are born with a true gift to instruct, motivate, and inspire.

As an answer to this problem, districts occasionally call on professional consultants to redo, revamp, recall, and reanalyze (and any other "re" you can think of) the teaching practices at the school. These consultants are paid thousands of dollars of taxpayers' money to stand in front of teachers, administrators, and other school personnel to impart their words of wisdom.

Tons of school money is being spent on training people in the ways of teaching. Universities, colleges, and other teacher-training facilities train teachers. After a teacher completes the requirements for teaching in the classroom, she receives a certificate. All training units require some fieldwork. This fieldwork (or clinical work) is an intense immersion of practice before the game.

When teachers attend staff development trainings, their specific needs are seldom met. Too often, schools fall into the trap of focusing on whatever is the current trend (buzzword) for that year. Usually, if a person can show data supporting his notion of a solution to a school problem, then the money starts pouring in—never mind the fact that the problem still exists when the consultant leaves.

There is not one state in this nation where you can apply for work as a teacher and not be exposed to "what's wrong with the school system" before the application process even begins. If you are lucky to be hired as a teacher, you will be in a school building with full administrative support. If you are lucky, you will be assigned to a school with adequate security.

More than likely, the assignment will be arranged for you, and you will take what you are given. The textbooks and theory classes that you will take in college and in alternative certification programs do not adequately discuss the reality of classroom experiences. Of course, nothing actually beats performing the task. However, there are matters at the very heart of surviving in the classroom that you must know. Those areas are addressed in later chapters.

At times, the reality of examining what's wrong with our schools sounds overwhelming. Before you get too discouraged, stick with understanding the nature of the problem. We must first scrutinize the root of education, how the philosophy of teaching has changed, and exactly why we insist on education for our children. For starters, we have to take a trip down memory lane. History will show us if we are moving forward, remaining stagnant, or not moving at all.

Besides the bureaucracy of the system, you will have to face students who now value obtaining an education less and less every day. It's this value component that is the key to improving the overall success of our students. Without understanding this ingredient, we are just throwing resources to the wind.

As you take a closer look at the influences from individuals and groups on education, you will conclude that the structure of education in this country needs to address the core value of what truly makes the difference: equality. It is difficult to imagine how a solution is possible if we use our resources to focus on anything but this central core issue.

Let's be clear. Money does not bring equality. Money can only build the buildings, furnish the playgrounds, and purchase classroom supplies. It cannot buy fair, caring, and gifted teachers.

Today's classrooms are filled with different kinds of children. It's important that educators keep abreast of these changes, meaning social media and technology. Some scholars profess to have the magic bullet that will answer the current problems of dropout rates, violence in classrooms, and achievement gaps.

Let's make the assumption that if more people were aware of what really goes on in schools, attracting committed teachers to the classroom would never be a problem. This book will attempt to propose that good teachers do exist, but that we miss identifying these gifted people and as a result are left with people who respond well to training. These trained individuals do nothing more than regurgitate information. They contribute to our attrition rates and violence in the classroom—in turn, leaving us footing the bill.

These people (good people) are sufficient, but not extraordinary. They do little to contribute to the welfare of lifelong learners. Here, you will find a blueprint to use to identify and groom those people who really have what it takes to make a difference in today's classrooms.

Teachers have such a tremendous responsibility. Teachers are in charge of our children for most of the daylight hours and sometimes into the evening. We should put forth all of our energy into guaranteeing that our children have the right person standing in front of them as motivators as well as instructors.

When we take a serious look at the entire school picture, we see that students have become victims of dissection and doom. Experts in the field ask: What do we do next? Better yet: How did we get here in the first place?

> Students have become victims of dissection and doom.

But have we become victims of our own lack of meta-cognition? How did I learn? How do I know what I know? That is what schools concentrated on not that long ago. We have abandoned that common-sense type of approach that could help lead our children into future competitive roles.

We abandoned that approach for a more elaborate and shinier approach. Somewhere along the line, we became overly excited about the age of technology. Educators thought they had to completely change the entire educational system in order to keep up with the fast pace of modern technology.

It's hard to pinpoint when the education system dug itself into the ground, because the system has been captive to political leadership that fluctuates between one ideology and the next, depending on who is in power.

What's true is that the topic of education, over the past few decades, has become extremely political. The matter has turned into a platform piece and can be used as a tool through which votes are generated. As long as this strategy works, the education platform has the potential to be abused.

Now people are scrambling to make things right. In the meantime, there are about twenty years of students roaming around with hardly an eighth-grade education and another huge chunk who are not marketable material. There is absolutely no way to recapture these people and put them in a better place. So we are working backwards in order to move forward. In effect, that process will take at least another twenty years in the absence of radical overhaul.

> We have abandoned that common-sense type of approach
> that could help lead our future generations.

It is mindboggling to think that what we left behind is what truly worked. The only component to add to what we already had was the technology piece. Despite the ebb and flow of political views, we had a value for knowledge in this country. The overall schematic to teaching was solid. There was a solid foundation.

Despite the efforts of some leaders to correct the unequal position between minorities and whites during the civil rights era, our nation has consistently pulled back on strides toward teaching tolerance to our children. The children from the 1960s are grown up. Many of these people are teachers. They can attest to the fact that little has changed.

Our nation has laws, but the laws are not the issue. The issue is perception and acceptance as equal partners. Minorities do not feel as though they stand on the same playing field as whites. This is evident in the types of careers they choose and the types of leadership positions they hold. We celebrate having a chief executive officer of a major food chain decades after the restaurant began.

We celebrate having minority sports coaches after years of being locked out of the meetings. This nation, in order to be competitive, must relieve itself of the ills of the past to move on. This is the only way our challenges in education will dissipate—for children know the difference.

A few experts have defined "new" methods (e.g., teacher evaluation techniques, classroom management) that influenced a new pedagogical approach to a substantial degree. About twenty years ago, the paradigm shifted in the direction of catering to the student. Teachers were no longer evaluated on their methods, but rather on the responses of the students. To some degree, this is good, because the students are the clients.

In a more general examination of the merit of this approach, it would seem more beneficial to continue observing the teacher. The assumption here would be that if the teacher is competent, then the clients will follow. Now, some experts may disagree. In that regard, it may be wise to look at the data to see how well the current method of accountability is working.

Research has been done on children and their learning habits. In the late 1950s, the ideology connecting poverty to intelligence was born. Since then, of all the philosophies regarding how children learn, this seems to be the hardest one to change. This old thinking is still hanging around today. Just recently, a report (Harvard University's *Dropout Nation*) was published indicating that poverty has nothing to do with academic achievement, as was once believed.[1]

The point is that we should stop thinking that poverty has anything to do with intelligence as immediately as possible. This idea is one of the heaviest weights holding back the advancement in our education system.

Good education is becoming like the dinosaur: extinct. If we are not careful, we will have generations of people who cannot function in society at all. Taxpayers will foot the bill for the uneducated generation coming down the road. So, for those concerned about us passing our debt down to our children and grandchildren, education must be considered a top priority.

There are already thousands of young people who are growing up without fundamental skills. For instance, how many of you realize that for a large number of public school students, misspelling a word no longer counts against the grade?

If you are shocked, then you should be. Some schools have gone as far as to fill in the child's name, address, school identification number, gender, and other personal information on standardized scoring sheets with the excuse that students cannot follow directions. Are we so overly concerned with student achievement that we dumb down education in the process?

The vicious cycle continues. If spelling does not count, then how can reading matter? Companies cannot hire people who cannot read or process information. That's a fact. On the other hand, children are only as smart as we allow them to be. One thing is clear—if the school districts across the nation do not get a handle on this, then we are all in big trouble. In general, districts are reacting instead of being proactive.

Credit must be given to those stepping out of the regularly shaped boxes of the past to carve a new future of competency. But everybody must get on the same page. New frontiers have to be born out of these ashes if America is to assume its number-one position again.

Frontiers that include eliminating a hierarchical structure in public education, formulating research-based national standards, and implementing methods to identify gifted people suited specifically for the classroom would be a tremendous start. These changes would be a welcome relief for the currently overburdened educational structure.

History can verify for us that a lack of education leads to a stagnated economy. You don't need a degree to come to that conclusion. Some economists are even referring to education as the elephant in the room that nobody wants to talk about. Others are discussing education as a civil right.

When public education was started in this country, it was done so on the premise that an education would provide for a stronger economy and better citizens. Somewhere along the way, politics and greed got in the way and left the children behind. Experts in the education field argue that having a well-educated society helps the society to move forward. So why can't we move this mountain? Knowing the truth will be the first step in solving this problem.

Note: Galileo Galilee was jailed for his views of the true position of the earth in relationship to the sun. During his time, the church ruled how people thought. Galileo had enough courage to stick to his beliefs and the proof that he had regarding the position of all the planets. He claimed that the sun was the center of the universe, not the earth. How could the truth be jailed? Sooner or later, the truth will be revealed. That is also a law of nature.

NOTE

1. "Harvard Education School Profs to poor and minority kids: You don't deserve college prep education" on Drop Out nation: Coverage of the reform of American public education blog, ed. RiShawn Biddle. www.dropoutnation.net/2011/02/02/harvard-graduate-school-education-poor-minority-kids-deserve-college-prep-education/

I
ENTER REALITY

1

Your New Name

"Everybody is a genius. But if you judge a fish by its ability to climb a tree, it will live its whole life believing that it is stupid."

—Einstein

You just received your passing scores to become a certified teacher (until the rules change), and you are excited to start the school year with a brand-new classroom and large boards—just like you imagined. The roster is in your mailbox, and you prepare for each little darling to enter the room on the first day.

BITCH

Wake up! You now have a new name. Your name is *bitch, bastard, heifer, gal,* or worse. How could this be, when they look so innocent? Are you thin-skinned? Can you take it without losing your cool? Even in the best of classrooms, you will have this experience if you stick around long enough.

Take it from a veteran: Don't befriend your students! This is the Golden Rule of teaching. You are not in the classroom to make friends with your students. You are hired to teach—period. Too often, new teachers, especially, try to overcompensate for their lack of experience by being overly friendly with their students.

This could be a drastic mistake. If you don't believe this, try doing it, and you will find yourself in your supervisor's office very quickly—or worse, unemployed. Children will tell lies about you. They create conspiracy groups that decide how they will take you down. It's a cultural thing.

Fairness matters to children. They are extremely observant. So it's always best to treat all students the same and not show any favoritism. The average child can talk on the phone, listen to music, and play video games at the same time. It takes a lot of different brain cells to multitask like that. It's commendable as well. So, treat them as if they *can* do, as if they *can* perform, as if they *can* succeed.

At first, you will be shocked. If you are anywhere close to normal, you will be shocked. Your first reaction will be: Can he really say that to me and get away with it? Sure he can. Even the elementary kids catch on quickly. The special education component of public education has stretched teachers to the limit. These rules and regulations alone have driven teachers away.

The teachers who leave the classroom in under five years often make claims that student discipline was the sole determining factor responsible for them leaving the classroom. You truly have to be a "Houdini" to teach a class with at least twenty different Individual Education Plans (IEPs) at one time, along with gifted students who deserve a more challenging environment. It's truly a juggling act.

The Psychology 101 classes cover special-needs students. What the books fail to give is the real life experiences. Theory makes good knowledge for the certification test, but life after the test requires knowledge of the real world. You will probably be asked to do student teaching. This gives you somewhat of a heads-up. Student teaching is analogous to taking a beginner's swim class, and full-time teaching is like swimming in the Olympics. Those are two totally different things. There will be every kind of child in your classroom. (See the part of the book that describes what the typical schoolchild looks like.) A child's behavior plays a very significant part in teaching.

You will be confronted with hard-to-reach students. Every year, the accommodations for special needs grow longer and longer. Is there a stretch limit? A true and sobering fact: From 1997 to 2001, teachers were the victims of approximately 1.3 million nonfatal crimes at school. These crimes included 817,000 thefts and 473,000 violent crimes (National Center for Educational Statistics).[1] At some point, you are likely to say, "Sit down and shut up!"

A blog post from *Education Week Teacher* by Louis C. (April 17, 2008) reads:

> There have been thousands of articles and discussions about violence in our schools yet there has been little or no information about what teachers are to do when confronted with an attack on a student or themselves. I was involved in hundreds of assaults in my career and I paid for training to deal with the physical aspects of violence. I am in the process of dealing with the NEA on teacher training to deal with assaults. This court recognized training is critical

to all educators in an increasingly violent atmosphere in our schools. Don't expect school boards or administrators to do anything for teachers because of fear of litigation. Teachers and our unions need to draw the line in the sand and prepare educators to deal with the dysfunctional atmosphere in schools.[2]

You must demand order and structure in your classroom. Without it, you will not be able to teach anything to anyone! This "demanding" is not damning. This "demanding" revolves around your presence. Do you have a demanding presence?

This is the key to being in control of the process. Teaching a child anything is a process. Even if you teach a child how to ride a bicycle, it takes a few times wobbling down the street and a couple of falls before she can ride all by herself.

Teaching takes patience. Those rough days when you may be cramping or dealing with a bad cold will occur. Be ready. How do you combat these times while maintaining professionalism? It is hard. The best advice is to breathe. The next part is to expect these incidents to take place at any given time. Students bring their problems and lay them at your feet. Teachers wear many hats.

Remember, there are a few "lawyers" in every class, or at least one parent every year. They know the rule book better than you do. They can probably cite references and dates of precedent cases. So treat them as if they know. Don't feel guilty for being firm. Children want to be disciplined.

The Archbishop of New Orleans wanted to do away with corporal punishment in a well-known all-male Catholic school, St. Augustine High School. The students collectively fought against the ruling to stand by the policy that had been a part of the school since its inception. Now, some people may see these students as totally bizarre, and others may be of the opinion that these are children and that they have to abide by the ruling.

The funny thing is that these young men recognize what's working at their school. They stated on national news that the unique discipline at the school is what separates them from the rest of the pack. The school has an impeccable record of achievement. Evidently, the students wanted to hold on to that reputation.

Students will rant and rave when you stand your ground, but it's what they truly respect. And that's where you want them to be. Continue with fair routines, operating as if everyone is cooperating. It's a matter of power. You have to win! Once a teacher enters a classroom, the power struggle begins. It may be a tug of war with the parents, the students, or both. The staff handbook should be memorized. The rules and regulations should be part of a regimental routine.

During the opening day ceremonies, make sure that you get the grassroots canvassing going strong. Your campaign should include: *The rules will be enforced. The rules will be followed. For instance, no one sits at the teacher's desk.* Allow a pause to discuss this point.

Some teachers allow students to go in their desk drawers, look through desk drawers, and sit at the teacher's desk. When you go into the room to be seen by the doctor, do you sit where the doctor sits? The point is that you are in a *teaching* environment. Teachers should not want to miss an opportunity to teach a child what is right. A small act of sitting at the teacher's desk can blow up to tremendous liberties, which the child may not be ready to handle.

There is no other option than fairness. Fairness is critical to teaching. Children will respect you if you are a fair person. No one gets over the other. Create an environment of trust, and you will be able to teach a child anything.

Build solid and sincere relationships with your students that do not involve anything personal. Keep pictures of you and the family at home. Some of you cannot imagine what harm this could do to a child. Well, consider this. Suppose you have a student in the classroom with a weird sense of reality. He is not loved at home and is anxious to come to school just to get away from home. These types of students look for attention. You might be the teacher that he decides to like. But there's a problem. He may perceive that you care for someone else more. Yes, this all sounds like a horror story. Nonetheless, these are just a few things to know. The primary order of business is that you are in the classroom to teach.

> Create an environment of trust, and
> you will be able to teach a child anything.

Be armed with insight. There is a very diverse psyche out there. So don't fool yourself into thinking that students don't know what's going on. Your students are on the computers at a young age. It's a different time than twenty years ago. Acknowledge that. Receive that. Embrace that. You are in the classroom to conduct business. It's a service industry. As a teacher, you have patrons who you must service—equally.

It's always business. It's never personal.

Make certain that you don't take your new name personally. These rules should govern you as well as the students. Let the name calling roll off of your shoulders. Don't get too wound up in the drama of the classroom, but don't let things "slide" either.

You may find yourself attending workshops at which consultants tell the audience that the best way to handle a child who calls you a name is to exhibit calm behavior and speak softly to the student. This type of response breeds negative feedback, because disruptive students perceive this as a weakness. So do you fight fire with fire? That's the $64,000 question. Well, the answer is: sometimes.

You call it. As in any other situation, use your inner gut feeling. This doesn't mean that you have to get in a student's face and become overly combative. What it implies is that you should not let anything just pass by. Some situations merit an immediate fix. Set your boundaries without fear. Students can smell fear. They will play on your emotions. They will do anything to break you down, because they don't want to be in school.

Most students arrive at school with very limited skills. Teachers are taught to follow a certain script. This script may not correspond to the students' true skills.

> Be armed with insight.

On the other hand, some students misbehave because they are not being challenged. If you dig deeply enough, you will find some bright minds out there. Teachers cannot physically approach a child, but there are ways to make them feel as if you had. Here are a few tips:

1. Make sure that you document everything. Let them know that you are keeping a file.
2. State your case on day one. Don't allow them to leave the class period not understanding the rules of *your* game.
3. Try a variety of different approaches. No one approach is sacred. Take the pulse of your classroom, like a doctor takes your vital signs.
4. Make parent contact from day one. It is imperative that you make your mark.
5. Learn names early on. Put faces with names within the first three days of school.
6. Call on students when they least expect it (random selection). Let them know that you have eyes in the back of your head.
7. Learn the signs: body language, types of walking, and eye movement psychology. In order to service these students, you have to know your audience. Knowing your audience is like entrepreneurs needing to know their target market. Set a ROI (Return on Investment) goal for your target audience. You have to be street smart.
8. Be assertive.
9. Be clear and concise at all times.
10. Stick to a routine.

A good teacher will set boundaries, stick to her guns, and make life livable for everybody concerned.

Remember, you have to live with "these people" for about 180 days. That's a long time. You want to be able to just look at your students and have them understand what's on your mind. How do you do that?

Train them by telling them and showing them what "the look" looks like. They may not come from homes where people have taught them what to expect. They may come from homes where the parents are not concerned about their future and where discipline is not high on the priority list.

You can tell them what you like to see done in the classroom. Be clear and concise. Routines cut down on inappropriate classroom behavior. It's like a law: if you run a red light, you pay the consequences.

Let them know that. It's all about respect.

> A good teacher will set boundaries, stick to her guns, and make life livable for everybody concerned.

Remember to keep your guard up. In today's computer language, keep a high firewall around you. A classroom is no personal forum.

Respect the students—no matter how angry you get with any of them. Remember that they belong to someone else, and you don't have to take them home with you. Yeah!

There will be trying times. What will you do? Make good judgment calls. One of the most important rules in the lifesaving book for swimmers says: It's better to save one life than to lose two. What that means is: if you don't know any lifesaving techniques, don't try to save someone who's drowning. It makes sense. Call someone who does.

NOTES

1. National Center for Educational Statistics (1997–2001), "Indicators of School Crime and Safety, 2010: Indicator 2: Incidence of Victimization at School and Away From School," http://nces.ed.gov/programs/crimeindicators/crimeindicators2010/ind_02.asp

2. Anthony Rebora, "A Student-Violence Epidemic," *Education Week Teacher*, April 15, 2008, http://blogs.edweek.org/teachers/webwatch/2008/04/an_epidemic_of_student_violenc.html

2
Defend Yourself

Some students may try to physically hit you. It may be due to a student's exceptionalities or just plain "I don't care attitude" about life. Whatever the reason, teachers today find themselves in precarious positions daily. Some of you will land in a combat zone. If you research the latest videos on YouTube, you will see that students do fight teachers (and vice versa).

Students will try to place you in a position where tempers will flare. One day you might not be feeling well, or you might be going through a personal hardship, and your patience level might be down. Know your limitations. You are human, and it's important to allow your students an opportunity to realize that good and bad days are a part of life. Faking it will only get you in more trouble.

A student should never address you outside of your formal name. You should put in place parameters so that this seldom happens. If a student becomes disrespectful, make sure that you follow the lines of protocol. Also, be wary of those who know the protocol and are misbehaving just to get out of the class. They know the drill. It's all part of their master plan.

The last thing they want is to be inside of the classroom. So, you will need to be extremely creative for these students. What does that mean? Creativity plays a huge role in running a safe environment. General rules are just that—generic. There is not a one-size-fits-all solution.

The methods of dealing with problems should be at least as varied as the types of students in the classroom. It's hard to explain what to do when the time comes. Rely on your gut. Humans are built with some instinctive qualities.

Use them to your advantage. What would you do if a student approached you to physically harm you? What would you do if the student had a weapon? What are your options?

Wherever you obtain your information, statistics do not replace experience "on the ground." These numbers reflect what is reported. A great number of unsafe conditions go unreported, because these numbers count against the school score.

Every year, schools are evaluated on their yearly performance. If the safety numbers are negative, the amount of money a school receives decreases, along with the school's ratings. As indicated, fighting is on the rise, especially in some sub-population groups. Now, what this translates into (in real life) is that physical confrontation is going to be a reality in your classroom.

If you talk to some veterans of the classroom, you will find that this type of violence is no longer found in large numbers just at the high school level, but in the lower grades as well. Different groups attempt to pin the blame on the movie industry, lack of parental control, video games, and a variety of other factors. The reason does not matter. Frankly speaking, when fights occur in the classroom, a teacher does not have time to think about statistics. At that point, it's a matter of survival.

Law enforcement personnel train teachers to recognize signs of possible adverse behavior before it occurs. This is extremely important. For instance, a student may make a sexual comment towards you just to get a reaction. The best response is always to follow the law and the policy of the school.

The minute you engage yourself in a verbal dialogue, you have lost the battle. From that moment on, other students will push the envelope, and you will see that you were instrumental in creating a hostile class setting.

You will not win over every student. Resign yourself to that fact before setting one foot inside of a classroom.

THE TYPICAL CLASSROOM

The number of students will vary from classroom to classroom. The types of students may lean more heavily to one side or the other, depending on the school's demographics.

In any one day, a teacher has to:

- Plan lessons
- Answer calls to the office
- Contact parents
- Guard behavior/speech
- Make accommodations for *all* students

	Anywhere				On school property			
Student characteristic	0 times	1 to 3 times	4 to 11 times	12 or more times	0 times	1 to 3 times	4 to 11 times	12 or more times
Total	68.5	24.0	5.0	2.6	88.9	9.6	0.9	0.6
Sex								
Male	60.7	28.4	6.9	4.0	84.9	12.8	1.2	1.0
Female	77.1	19.1	2.8	1.0	93.3	6.0	0.5	0.2
Race/ethnicity[1]								
White	72.2	22.0	3.8	1.9	91.4	7.7	0.5	0.4
Black	58.9	29.9	7.5	3.7	82.6	14.9	1.4	1.0 !
Hispanic	63.8	26.5	6.8	3.0	86.5	11.4	1.3	0.8
Asian	81.1	13.8	2.2	2.9	92.3	5.6	0.8 !	1.2 !
American Indian/Alaska Native	57.6	23.3	9.6	9.6	79.3	18.9	‡	‡
Pacific Islander/Native Hawaiian	67.4	17.7	6.8	! 8.0 !	85.2	9.4	3.7 !	‡
Two or more races	65.8	25.9	5.2	3.0	87.6	10.5	1.2 !	0.7 !

Table 2.1 Percentage of students in grades 9–12 who reported having been in a physical fight during the previous 12 months, by location, number of times, and selected student characteristics: 2009

! Interpret data with caution.
‡ Reporting standards not met.
[1] Race categories exclude persons of Hispanic ethnicity.
Note: "On school property" was not defined for survey respondents. The term "anywhere" is not used in the YRBS questionnaire; students are simply asked how many times in the last 12 months they had been in a physical fight. Detail may not sum to totals because of rounding.
SOURCE: Centers for Disease Control and Prevention, National Center for Chronic Disease Prevention and Health Promotion, Youth Risk Behavior Surveillance System (YRBSS), 2009.

- Consistently assess if *all* students are learning
- Clean up after activities
- Correct papers
- Input grades and other data

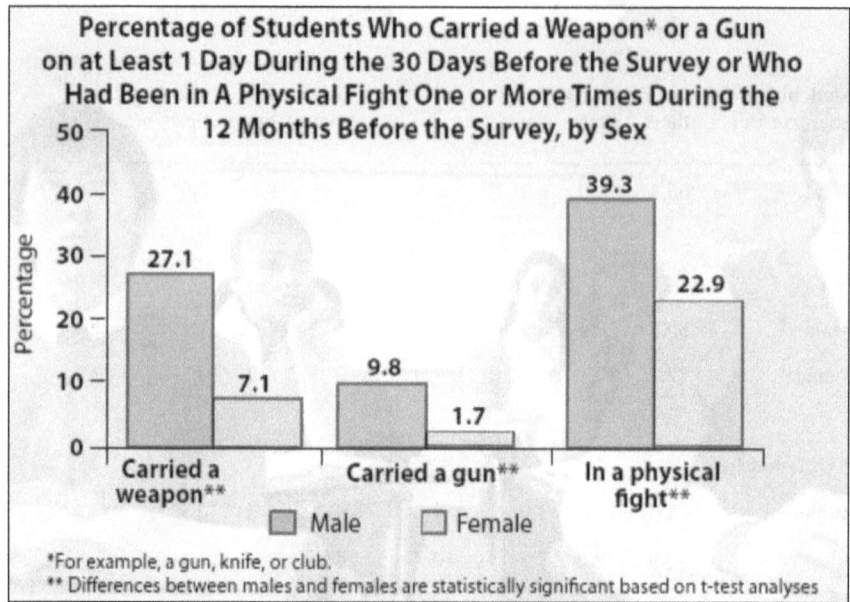

Figure 2.1
Source: Centers for Disease Control and Prevention, Youth Risk Behavior Surveillance System (YRBSS), 2009 National Youth Risk Behavior Survey Overview.

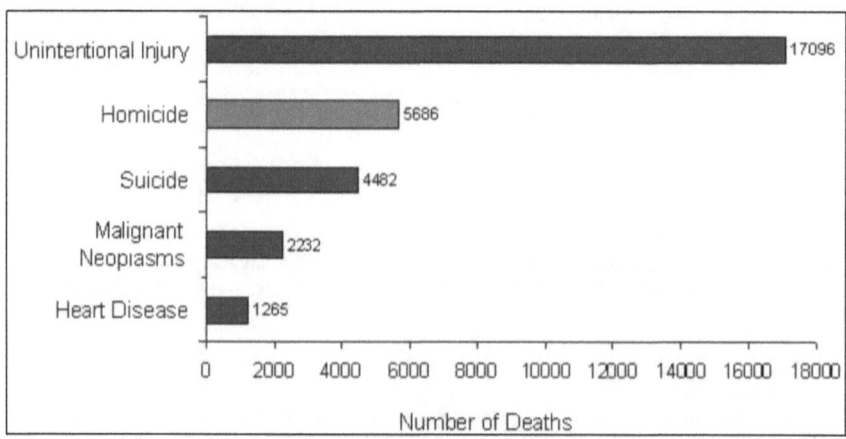

Figure 2.2 Five Leading Causes of Deaths among Persons Ages 10–24 Years, United States, 2005.
Source: Youth Violence: National Statistics Leading Causes of Death
http://www.cdc.gov/ViolencePrevention/youthviolence/stats_at-a_glance/lcd_10-24.html

- Attend meetings
- Answer emails
- Create tests, activities, quizzes, and other assessments

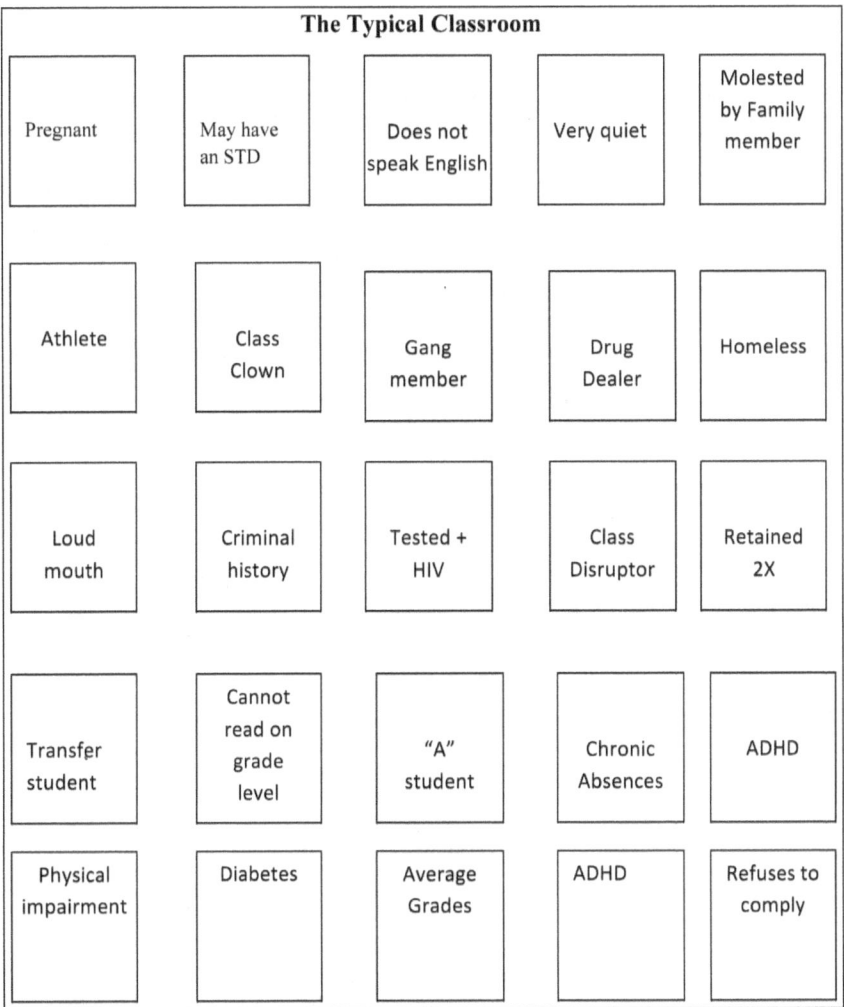

Figure 2.3 The Typical Classroom
(Order of seating does not indicate actual positions.)

- Take care of sick children
- Duty (may include breaking up fights)
- Issue hall passes
- Supervise for safety
- Take and report attendance
- Meet with fellow teachers

Let's take a look at the reality of each of your classroom categories.

Pregnancy

The number of pregnancies is an issue for schools. It stands to reason that if pregnancies occur, then teenagers are having unprotected sex. Therefore, sexually transmitted diseases are a given. This should not be a surprise.

This is such a problem that international organizations are trying to influence the knowledge base for teens regarding sexual health information. Teachers are not able to advise students on their sexual behavior. No matter how strong the temptation to voice your personal opinion, the law is in favor of the parents. However, if you are a teacher at the middle school or high school level, the probability of having a pregnant student in your class is pretty high.

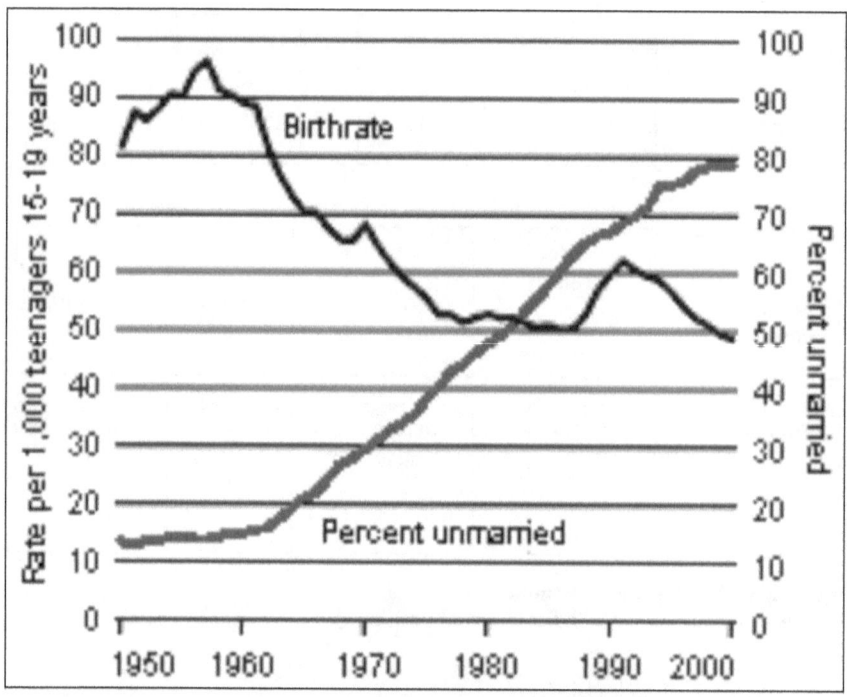

Figure 2.4 Births to Teenagers in the United States, 1940–2000
In 2006, 750,000 women younger than twenty became pregnant.
Source: National Center for Health Statistics, "Births to Teenagers in the United States, 1940–2000," *National Vital Statistics Report,* 2001, Vol. 49, No. 10.

Gangs

Of the one million gang members, about 40 percent are juveniles.[1] Gang members can be huge headaches at schools, to say the least. Whatever happens on the outside is certain to spill over into the school environment. The sole purpose for gang members coming to school is to recruit. This undercurrent is extremely difficult to identify and eradicate. This group makes up a significant component of the fabric of America's public school system.

Children who may not be exposed to gang activity where they reside risk being exposed to gang activity while at school. There is really no way to escape it. School administrators cannot get control of this problem fast enough. Gang members prepare their plans ahead of time. They know the routines of teachers, and they are well aware the nature of the school building.

This challenge begs the question: How safe are our schools? There is no doubt that gang violence has a direct connection to victimization and bullying.

Homelessness

The statistics are in: As of 2002, there are 1,682,900 homeless and runaway youth in our country.[2] This number reflects the state of our economy, as well as children who are victims of family issues. Homeless children feel trapped. At times, class discussions such as "What did your family do for the holidays?" or "When you go home tonight, watch the evening news" may pop up. These types of discussions and assignments may be threatening and offensive to children who do not have a specific place to lay their heads. Teachers have to be extremely sensitive to guard their speech and to assign work that can be accomplished by all students.

Homeless children are not going to be wearing a T-shirt saying: "I'm Homeless!" If the student is the victim of a fire or a natural disaster, the school may be allowed to share the information with the teacher. Otherwise, teachers do not know who has a home and who does not.

Drug Dealers

Count on someone in the classroom being a drug dealer. The school is his playground. It is where he traffics his goods and collects his money. This person is not always a male. Females are actively involved as well.

Most of our schools are filled with "structural gaps"—locker rooms, space between buildings, stadiums, and parking lots. No amount of law enforcement can be everywhere all at once. Students outnumber teachers on an average of 20:1. Drug dealers work very effectively and efficiently throughout the school.

The other students know who they are. In today's world, snitching is considered a cop-out. To gather information from other students is next to impossible. The only way drug dealers are exposed is to actually catch them while in the act. How hard is that? Drug dealers are a standard part of too many American school campuses.

HIV

Young Americans between the ages of thirteen and twenty-four are still contracting HIV at the rate of two per hour. Each year three thousand adolescents contract sexually transmitted diseases, which is about one in four sexually experienced teens.[3]

Because of privacy laws, teachers are not permitted to know which students have the HIV infection. Teachers receive limited training on handling these cases. The most a classroom might receive is a "safety bucket" containing a flashlight, kitty litter, a shower curtain, and some gloves. The best line of defense is for teachers to make themselves aware of the probability of having an HIV-positive child in the classroom and to operate accordingly.

Not all school administrators enjoy talking to their staff about the reality of HIV at their school. As alarming as the statistics are, who can afford not to?

Loudmouths/Class Clowns

Some people are just born entertainers. Adult comedians are asked, "Were you like this in school?" The answer is a resounding "Yes." It stands to reason that a classroom environment cannot survive a continual flow of antics. Nothing would get accomplished. So, what is the best way to handle these students, while still teaching the rest of the class? At an early age, these children recognize their gift. The challenge is to teach them how to temper it without diminishing their love for attention and laughter. The best approach is to let them be who they are.

These are strong personalities. So putting up opposition only leads to a power struggle. Teachers should keep them busy and allow them to work their magic. It's these students who help the most. They are leaders, and they are not afraid of showing it.

Molestation

Molestation is a prevalent crime that goes completely unnoticed too frequently. Teachers, by law, must report any suspicion of child abuse to school authorities, as well as to the local police department. Here are some signs of molestation:

- Changes in behavior, such as withdrawal, fearfulness, crying without provocation
- Change in eating habits
- Disrupted sleep patterns, fear of the dark, or nightmares
- Regression to more infantile behavior, such as bedwetting, sucking their thumbs, or abnormal and excessive crying
- Bruises, rashes, cuts, limping, or poorly explained injuries
- Vaginal or rectal bleeding, pain, itching, swollen genitals, vaginal discharge, or sexually transmitted diseases
- Stained or torn underwear
- Unusual interest in or knowledge of sexually related matters, or expression of affection in ways inappropriate for a child of that age
- Fear of a person or an intense dismay at being left somewhere or with someone (relatives, babysitters, etc.)
- Other behavioral signals, such as aggressive or disruptive behavior, running away, failing in school[4]

If teachers pay close attention, they should be able to detect the silent screams of molested students. Students may play out their secret in a variety of ways.

- Approximately 4,300 child molesters were released from prisons in fifteen states in 1994. An estimated 3.3 percent of these 4,300 were rearrested for another sex crime against a child within three years of release from prison.
- Among child molesters released from prison in 1994, 60 percent had been in prison for molesting a child thirteen years old or younger.
- Offenders who had victimized a child were on average five years older than the violent offenders who had committed their crimes against adults. Nearly 25 percent of child victimizers were age forty or older, but about 10 percent of the inmates with adult victims fell in that age range.[5]

Teacher observed characteristics of molested students:

Girls	Boys
- Plays with hair constantly	- Picks fights
- Picks fights	- Makes "smart" remarks
- Gets very upset if one hair is out of place	- Stays in trouble at school
- Frequent trips to restroom	- Withdrawn
- Withdrawn	- Stomach aches

- Sudden weight loss/gain
- Uses excessive makeup
- Seeks affection from adults
- Does not dress out for P.E.
- Overly exposed clothing
- No interest in friends
- Overly friendly with boys
- Does not get report card signed
- May be an "A" student
- Hangs out after school
- Does not dress out for P.E.
- Brags about self
- Neatly dressed
- Sudden weight loss
- Quits everything
- Teases other students
- Compulsive neatness
- Resists close proximity

These characteristics do not cover the entire field of signs. However, they are a starting point. In general, children do not have the tools to cover up such a huge secret. If teachers build relationships with their classes, then the slightest change will be detected.

Criminal History

As stated in earlier tables and statistics, teenagers are committing a lot of crimes. Once again, teachers are not provided with a student's criminal record. To little or no avail, teachers have tried to file lawsuits against school districts to disclose the reason why the students were detained. These teachers have been turned down again and again. The probability of having a student with a criminal history in the classroom is high. And that's the bottom line.

Class Disruptors

Experts claim that class management is the remedy for students who disrupt the class. Actually, class management is only a small piece of the solution. Students who disrupt the classroom environment do what they do on purpose. This is not a haphazard occurrence. With that in mind, management ideas can lead to frustration. Frustration leads teachers to early exit from the classroom. Class disruptors have needs. The trick is finding out what those needs are. Inexperienced teachers certify this as probably the number one reason for leaving the profession. These students drain teachers. So staff development may not be the answer.

To combat these students is a mistake—in some instances. Class disruptors may indeed be the brightest students in the school. But who would know it? Peer pressure plays an important part in the lives of class disruptors. Class disruptors must be studied (observed) to find out what makes them tick. This is an exercise in mental gymnastics.

These students are also time consuming. While attention is being paid to the disruptors, the other students fall victim to lack of instruction. Teachers do not have time to waste on a few students. Overall school scores suffer because of a serious lack of skills in dealing with difficult students. These scores make it appear as if school personnel are not doing what they were hired to do.

Individuals as well as organizations have come up with quick-fix remedies. Some work. Some do not. The true answer to the problem will stand the test of time. Class disruptors actually help identify teachers who do not belong in the classroom. These students are a true teacher's litmus test.

There is no one way to deal with these students. The approach is like a gumbo recipe, and the ingredients are different for each student. Each class disruptor has his own fingerprint. One disruptor may require something as simple as a parent conference. Another disruptor may require an alternative school setting, along with prescribed counseling.

Class disruptors cannot be ignored. In some instances, it's these students who turn out to show the most commitment. If planned correctly, a teacher can turn these students into the people they are truly meant to be—leaders.

ADHD (Attention Deficit Hyperactivity Disorder)

As of 2007, approximately 9.5 percent of children between the ages of four and seventeen, or 5.4 million children, have been diagnosed with ADHD.[6] Teachers encounter millions of ADHD children every year; just as many may go undiagnosed. Once a child has been determined to be a candidate for the drugs that control ADHD, teachers must plan for accommodations.

Teachers who have a difficult time controlling their classrooms often think that a very active child must have a problem if he or she cannot sit still. Along with the millions of children who are diagnosed as having ADHD, many more are misdiagnosed. There is a wave of parents and physicians who are opposed to using drugs to "settle" children. Nutritionists think that a better diet can overcome the problem.[7]

The cogs of bureaucracy move very slowly in the school system. While teachers are waiting to get students serviced, the ADHD students are still inside of the classroom. In the meantime, the students have to be taught and business has to be as usual.

Registered Sex Offenders

Registered sex offenders are not always adults. School administrators must inform the teacher of the presence of a registered sex offender. However, this is not common knowledge. And if the teacher discloses this information, the consequence could be immediate dismissal. This is a serious situation and should not be taken lightly.

Quiet Students

What are they thinking? Quiet students can be grossly misinterpreted. The prognosis could go either way. The quality may be a cultural thing, or it could be the sign of a much deeper problem. The challenge is getting them to open up, because teachers need to know who they have in the classroom.

It is important for teachers to reach these students and to have some sort of handle on predictability. Staying in front of problems is almost the entire battle. There is no "best practice" to use here. Each student is unique. These students have to trust teachers. This challenge calls for creativity and patience.

"A" Students

Teachers have to accommodate accelerated students in the classroom.

Physically Impaired Students

Physically impaired students have an assigned aid. These students have the right to a free and equal education under the law. Any type of discrimination could result in major lawsuits. Under the Individuals Disabilities Act 1990, all public school buildings and classrooms must be equipped to accommodate the physically impaired student.

Teachers may or may not be given a heads-up about having a physically impaired student. Sometimes, the school authorities show up at the door with the student who requires a specific classroom setting (e.g., distance from the board, specific desk for wheelchairs, or enough chairs for the student and the aide).

This law has withstood the test of time. So it is important to note that there will be no circumventing this law.

Social Promotion

School success is dependent on every link in the chain. If there is one weak link anywhere along the way, the trickle-down effect could be disastrous. Social promotion occurs when a student is too old (in age) for the grade he is assigned to.

Teachers may have seventeen-year-olds in class with fourteen-year-old students. In the early years, a lot of children are retained in kindergarten.

This puts them behind before they start. These students enter the classroom at a disadvantage, and they are not happy about it.

The internal struggle is fitting into the crowd. Most retained students worry about what other people have to say. They think everyone knows, even though others may not be aware of the circumstances at all.

Parents or guardians must be involved in the child's plan. Even if the parents have to be enticed to come to the school, they must be involved in planning for their child's success. Because many children experience being retained at a young age, they tend to accept failure and even actually expect failure. They know that they have to work twice as hard just to be in the "right" place.

If the student is old enough, he should have input into the plan for graduating. There are many of ideologies behind the issue of social promotion. Proponents think that it will give the student time to master the subject. Opponents think that this does not help at all, because some children are late bloomers. And others feel that these students suffer at the hands of incompetent teachers.

Non-English Speakers

English is the official language of the United States. According to the 2000 United States Census, there were 215,423,557 people who claimed to be first-language English speakers and 35,964,744 who claimed to speak other languages besides English.[8]

In some states, Hispanics are quickly becoming the majority in public schools. No matter how good instruction is in the classroom, if communication is lacking, there can be no success. The facts are in front of us. Our system has to move swiftly to accommodate the culture and lifestyle of hundreds of thousands of children if it is to provide what they need in order to learn. Instead, too often these children are met with disrespect and intolerance.

If our teaching philosophy holds true for all students, then our system must embrace reality.

Diabetes

According to the Centers for Disease Control, about one out of four hundred to six hundred children has diabetes.[9] If you work at a school with at least four hundred children, the odds are that there are children with diabetes enrolled at the school. This means that a teacher must constantly be on the lookout for signs and symptoms of children who go undiagnosed.

Fatigue—might mean that the child is not being defiant if he sleeps in class.

Frequent urination—might mean that the child is sick, and not worrying the teacher about leaving the class for "no reason."
Frequent thirst—might mean that the child needs to get a sip of water more often than the rest of the class.
Blurred vision—might mean that the child is not taking notes not because he is being defiant, but because he can't see the board.
Frequent hunger—might mean that the child is not sneaking food from his book bag because he trying to be annoying, but because he has a glucose level problem.
Obesity—might mean that a teacher has to be acutely aware of bullying tactics.

If a teacher suspects any or all of these symptoms, then the school nurse should be notified. The nurse can then forward any concern to the child's parents.

Chronic Absences

By law (compulsory attendance laws), a child must physically be present in class 90 percent of the regular school year in order to receive credit for the class.[10] Most parents are aware of this requirement. It is important that teachers keep very detailed documents regarding student attendance. There may be times when an attendance record is involved with a legal case. Grade books and attendance books can be subpoenaed.

NOTES

1. http://www.helpinggangyouth.com/statistics.html
2. National Coalition for the Homeless, http://www.nationalhomeless.org/factsheets/youth.html
3. Office of National AIDS Policy: The White House, *Youth and HIV/AIDS 2000: A New American Agenda*, http://www.whitehouse.gov/administration/eop/onap
4. http://www.childmolestationvictim.com/signs.html
5. http://www.criminal-records.org/articles/criminal_offenders_stats.html
6. http://www.cdc.gov/ncbddd/adhd/data.html
7. http://mentalhealthmatters.com/index.php?option=com_content&view=article&id=236
8. "Language Use and English-Speaking Ability: 2000," Census 2000 Brief (October 2003).
9. Centers for Disease Control, http://www.cdc.gov/diabetes/pubs/factsheet11.htm
10. Compulsory Attendance Law, http://en.wikipedia.org/wiki/Compulsory_education

3
Do Our Standards Promote Equality?

> "I am only one, but still I am one. I cannot do everything, but still I can do something; and because I cannot do everything, I will not refuse to do something that I can do."
>
> —Helen Keller

The National Council for Accreditation of Teacher Education goes to great lengths to define, qualify, and prepare standards that help shape our education system in this country. The standards for teacher preparation are outlined every seven years, with thousands of pieces of input solicited from a variety of people.

The most recent documentation of standards (2008) is approximately ninety-eight pages long, including the glossary. It is important to note the frequency of reoccurring words in the latest edition of the document, as they relate to equality in the classroom (see table 3.1).

Notice that the most important words to teaching children are those words that occur least frequently. Shouldn't that be the other way around? This observation is not to diminish the enormous work done by this agency. There are many instances where synonyms and other ways of describing concepts like *equality* and *fairness* are used. What is noteworthy is that the words that should define what we view as important in our country are, in reality, last on the list. No one can argue the fact that professional knowledge and skills define what teachers can offer to students.

It is a given that people who wish to teach know and understand what they want to teach. The public is reassured about this through methods of teacher certification.

Table 3.1

Term	Frequency used (approx.)
Professional Disposition	102
(Professional) Knowledge and Skills	100
All students learn	27
Fairness	18
Teacher preparation	13
Caring	8
Equal	4
Social justice	2
Competent	2

The point is that our classrooms should be based on equality. Yet our standards stress "professional disposition" and "knowledge and skills." Of course, no one would argue with the fact that these qualities are extremely important, and everything should be done to include them. But, fairness and equality should count more. How do you train someone to care? How do you know if someone really cares or if they are faking it?

That is the question at the heart of our challenge to educate all children. Philosophically, a person either has a caring character or does not. Caring is an intrinsic model developed from a young age. It is a quality built upon a system of values. For instance, consider these cases: Would you pick up a piece of paper from the floor if no one were around? Or, would you behave the same way in private as you do in public?

Caring breeds fairness. A caring person cannot help but judge fairly. It comes with the territory. Yet we deal with black-and-white lists to evaluate the institutions that churn out our teachers.

We set standards according to what the public can understand, what the public likes. Most times, tradition is hailed over change and innovation. Somehow, the idea that caring and fairness bring equality makes us feel uncomfortable. Our educational structure has no other alternative but to meet the new challenges of global competition honestly.

For at least a century, our nation has been struggling to provide an equal, competitive, and quality education for all students. Why is it that one hundred years is not long enough to solve a problem? In the world of science, when an experimental design proves fruitless, the procedure and the hypothesis are changed.

Maybe the question is wrong. Have we been asking the wrong question all this time? Certainly, we are stuck at the collecting data stage. Over the years, failed attempts have morphed into more problems. Now instead of just one problem, we have several. Here are a couple of errors we have made while waiting for real answers:

1. Money will solve our education problem.
2. Rigorous teacher preparation/evaluations lead to increased student success.
3. Disparities will persist regardless of any efforts.

Let's take a closer look at the last assumption. It is a quite subtle but extremely impactful notion that runs like a deep undercurrent in our educational system. Despite the efforts of thousands of learned people, it is an inner acceptance that the disparities will always be among us.

Yes, we have accepted the fact that there will be thousands of graduates every year from thousands of cities in America who will graduate with unequal standards of education. It is not a secret that some diplomas carry more weight than others. Why? Why don't all high school diplomas carry the same weight?

Have we accepted our prejudices to the point that we keep sweeping the problems under the rug, even though we are well aware that they still exist? How long are we going to turn our heads? How long can we afford to churn out generations of functionally illiterate people?

According to the philosophies regarding students for "human capital," the work force is extremely lacking in individuals who possess minimally adequate skills. The notion of our country becoming more competitive just got weaker.

Equality is unequivocally the single most important issue in American education today. There is much discussion about twenty-first-century schools and how they will look:

- Teachers as facilitators
- Open school buildings
- Global communication "ikids"

None of these things will prove fruitful if the people standing in front of the classroom are not intrinsically fair-minded people. Our initial hypothesis is that all children can learn. To some teachers, this statement generates a response of: "Are you crazy?"

Our education system loses thousands of well-trained individuals every year due to failed expectations. Just think of the millions of dollars spent training these teachers.

- Drop outs
- Teachers who leave the classroom

- Teacher staff development (training unrelated to real problem, time spent outside of the classroom)
- Inadequate inventory
- Lost/stolen equipment
- School corruption (thievery, nepotism, unfair hiring practices)
- Re-testing for certification

There are tons of certified teachers in our country who are not teaching. They found out through experience what should be taught in the first class of teacher candidate training: Not every one of you is meant to be a teacher. And, every effort should be made to weed these people out instead of training them to be someone they were never meant to be.

When college students express an interest in becoming a teacher, the training institution should immediately get a background statement that includes answers to the following questions:

1. How long have you wanted to teach?
2. Have you ever been around teachers (family or close friends)?
3. Do you know the beginning salary of teachers in your state?
4. Do you know your personality type?
5. How close are you to starting a family?
6. If a child proceeds to physically harm you, what would you do?
7. What did you want to be in third grade?
8. Are you going to change careers?

These questions should give anyone a good running start. If indeed training units are exercising methods similar to this, good. It is important to know one's inner self before entering the classroom. Effective teachers know themselves very well. Our standards dictate "professional disposition" and emphasize "knowledge and skills." Of course, there are thousands of mechanics, but how many of them do you trust to work on your car?

4

Who Needs Laws?

"A lie cannot live."

—Martin Luther King, Jr.

For some children, thinking about the end goal of having an education is like looking at a mirage. They feel helpless, despite the promises of education authorities. For most minorities in this country, the reality of not having these promises met is present each and every day.

Generational conversation cannot take place unless all those involved feel empowered. There cannot be any weak links in the chain. Our national attitude about making sure that every person receives an equal education must change.

Despite laws being in place, there are still too many children falling through the cracks. We don't need more laws. We need people in place with a different attitude about educating all children, removing as many biases as we possibly can. Teaching a child is easy if the child is receptive.

Going forward means that we get our act together. One segment of society cannot advance while the rest lies in waiting. In this country, we believe that every child deserves a free and equal education. No one has a problem with the "free" part. It's the "equal" part that's the problem. How can we ensure that each child can learn if our attitude is wrong?

Attacking this problem should be the focal point of every classroom, every school district, and every national office. If there is something (anything) that prevents a person from offering an equal education to all the children in the classroom, then that person should be removed. Those persons who have personalities that do not sincerely promote a child's well-being should get out of the business.

5

Does Certification Prepare You for the Classroom?

We could take some lessons from the Catholic model of education. Not all Catholic schools require state certification. Now, why pick this model? In scientific study, researchers learn about diseases by studying the abnormal. This is not to say that the Catholic model is abnormal. It is the opposite of what we use for public school education. That makes this model ideal for comparison.

Catholic schools experience great success in student achievement. Some experts claim that there are a variety of factors responsible for this success. Let's go back to the fact that not all teachers are certified. How could these schools experience so much success with their teachers and not impose the burden of receiving a state certificate?

Most certification programs take about two years to complete. Alternative certification programs require about one year. That's the fast track. Public schools require "highly qualified" status in order to continue employment. Is this a joke? Highly qualified? Yet the children fail.

National certification requires a lot of work. The tonnage of required documents should be able to help anyone make a case to defend a thesis for a Ph.D. degree. The work is incredibly intense. The work includes self-assessments. This is not a bad idea. Self-assessment is actually a powerful skill. The rest of the work includes reflective writing beyond belief. Both state certification programs and National Certification programs require you to take tests.

These tests cause some people a lot of grief. In some states, a significant number of people fail the certification test. The cost of the test averages $120.00 per attempt. You have to pay more for the digital versions. And this cost refers to each individual test in the chosen area of specialty. Every year there are thousands of people who fail these tests. In some states, more minorities fail the test than other test takers. This has become an issue.

Additionally, some states do not accept National Board Certification.[1] This should raise a red flag. Are states mainly using these tests to generate revenue? Testing companies pitch their bids before state boards in an effort to win contracts. These contracts are very lucrative. Somebody is making the money. The number of teachers who fail state tests has become a national embarrassment. How can a person successfully complete a certification program and fail the test, not once but multiple times?

It may not be the person, but the test that is the problem. Testing has been a certain turnoff for a lot of potentially great teachers. There is an issue here. If a person is apt enough to complete course work, how can she fail the test? That's the question at the heart of the matter regarding state testing, and testing for teaching at all. One thing is certain—the testing companies are making a lot of money.

If non-certified people can teach children who then outperform most public school children, then why do we hang on to insisting that public school teachers obtain certification? What we need are more competent teachers. Testing cannot identify what we need, unless we change the test. Do certification programs give us that?

This is where the Catholic schools leave the public schools: *Teachers who make the difference are those who answer the call to teach.* Catholic schools pay lower salaries than public schools. So it can't be the money teachers make. Parent involvement is not all of the answer as to why children are performing so well. It's not the tuition.

Some public schools have much better facilities than Catholic schools—tennis courts, gymnasiums, stages for performances, outdoor equipment. The main difference is the fact that non-public schools can teach about making good moral decisions. Without getting into the religion issue, it is important to note what a major difference this makes.

Every public school student, no matter the grade level, should take classes in value decision making. For instance, first graders can participate in responding to questions like: if no one is around on the playground and there is a piece of paper on the ground, would you pick it up?

Value teaching has to be an integral part of our curriculum, if our nation is serious about global competition. If children don't see the value of receiving an education, then they won't stick around for it. Talented teachers can make the difference. These teachers hold the key to turning our dismal statistics around.

How can we identify gifted people and encourage them to become teachers? Have you ever met someone and said to him or her, "You look just like a hairdresser, or a coach, or a teacher?" Allow me to ask you to think about what we trust as the "mother look," the "entertainer look," the "lawyer look."

People who answer their true calls in life become that role. A talented surgeon has special hands. Some call their hands "gifted." When musicians are self-taught, we celebrate that. We pay huge sums of money for good seats.

Let's look at the possibility that some gifts rub off. Every now and again we hear from famous singers who tell their stories. In a lot of cases, we hear that they are the products of parents who play music or sing as well. Maybe the genetic factor is in play here. Who knows? One thing that's true—being around someone who is gifted tends to give another person a tendency toward that gift. Of course, this is empirical knowledge.

The results are not. There are some people truly born to teach. No matter how many observations are made in the classrooms of these special people, those who are not born to teach will never be great teachers. It's that simple. No amount of training can resolve this issue. Programs to align how concepts are taught are a serious waste of time and money.

The people who are easy learners may continue teaching out of complacency. These people ride the system, but produce mediocre achievement. Mediocrity will not cut it. This nation needs excellence—in a hurry.

This gift cannot be taught to others. Can you imagine Michelangelo teaching art and expecting the same quality of murals? Books written about techniques in classroom teaching are doing nothing but perpetuating the notion that people can be taught to teach.

Making a difference in the schools today means that we locate, identify, and encourage gifted people to enter into the classroom. Religious orders have a variety of methods of identifying people who have the "call." Medical schools have methods of interviewing school candidates that let them know if they have a potential gifted doctor sitting in front of them.

Teaching is one of the most important jobs that we have in this country. Yet we have no component in place to determine if the candidate was born to teach. The criteria include: Have you passed the state test? Do you have a college degree? Do you have teaching experience? How long have you been a teacher? Instead, some of the following questions should be asked:

1. What did your parents do?
2. When you were in third grade, what did you want to be?
3. Did you ever play teacher as a child?
4. Did you go to school where your parents taught?
5. How many people in your family are teachers?
6. Can you imagine doing anything else in life besides teaching?

Be ready for a small pool of applicants. Here's the thing—there are a lot of people who were born to teach. They're just not answering the call—for a variety of reasons. Money is one of those reasons. The teacher's salary is one of the main obstacles preventing our schools from being filled with gifted people.

A person with a true command of her discipline can control a classroom, can impart knowledge, and can inspire. Every one of us can recall that one teacher who changed our lives. Did that person not stand out amongst the others?

Gifted teachers can identify others with the gift. That's one way in which we can keep teachers who keep this nation on top. In every grade, children should be encouraged to choose teaching as a career, and teachers should help to groom children who seem to have "it."

Parents who understand this seek schools where gifted teachers abound. These kinds of schools are usually too expensive for the majority of the public to afford. We can change that. We should change that. We cannot afford not to change this attitude. Our future as a nation depends on it.

If you think you are ready to enter the classroom, here are a few facts to consider. This is a glimpse of the typical student in America's schools today:

- 5.3 million children (three to seventeen years of age) with ADHD[2]
- 463,000 children in foster care[3]
- More than 20 million children on Medicaid[4]
- At least 23,000 privately insured children in the U.S. are now taking diabetes medications[5]
- 750,000 women under age twenty became pregnant (2006)[6]
- 19.3 abortions per 1,000 women for teenagers (2006)[7]
- One out of every 110 births is autistic[8]
- 7.1 million children currently have asthma[9]
- For the number of children with disabilities, see table 5.1
- For the number of children living in poverty, see table 5.2
- 4,043 children under thirteen years of age diagnosed with AIDS (2008)[10]
- 65,500 adopted children living with lesbian or gay parents (2007)[11]
- 2,154,000 children living with unmarried parents (2007)[12]
- One out of 50 children is homeless[13]
- 771,700 children are victims of neglect[14]
- 135,000 children are victims of sexual abuse[15]
- 148,500 children are victims of emotional abuse[16]
- 3 million children have incarcerated parents[17]
- 8,000 teens become infected every day with a sexually transmitted disease[18]
- One to two out of 100,000 children under age fifteen will commit suicide[19]
- 22 million children (three to eleven years old) are exposed to secondhand smoke[20]

Table 5.1 Percentage distribution of students 6 to 21 years old served under Individuals with Disabilities Education Act, Part B, by educational environment and type of disability: Fall 2007

Type of disability	All environments	Regular school, time outside general class — Less than 21 percent	Regular school, time outside general class — 21–60 percent	Regular school, time outside general class — More than 60 percent	Separate school for students with disabilities	Separate residential facility	Parentally placed in regular private schools[1]	Homebound/ hospital placement	Correctional facility
All students with disabilities	**100.0**	**56.8**	**22.4**	**15.4**	**3.0**	**0.4**	**1.1**	**0.4**	**0.4**
Specific learning disabilities	100.0	59.0	29.7	9.2	0.6	0.1	0.9	0.2	0.4
Speech or language impairments	100.0	86.7	5.7	4.5	0.3	#	2.8	0.1	#
Mental retardation	100.0	15.8	27.6	49.0	6.0	0.4	0.3	0.5	0.3
Emotional disturbance	100.0	37.3	19.7	24.1	13.1	2.1	0.4	1.2	2.0
Multiple disabilities	100.0	12.9	16.1	45.2	20.6	1.9	0.5	2.5	0.3
Hearing impairments	100.0	51.9	17.6	16.8	8.0	4.3	1.1	0.2	0.1
Orthopedic impairment	100.0	50.0	17.4	24.5	5.5	0.2	0.9	1.5	0.1
Other health impairments[2]	100.0	59.0	25.4	11.7	1.6	0.2	1.0	1.0	0.3
Visual impairments	100.0	60.1	14.3	12.9	6.3	4.5	1.3	0.6	0.1
Autism	100.0	34.6	18.2	36.9	8.7	0.7	0.6	0.3	#
Deaf-blindness	100.0	20.8	13.8	32.4	21.2	9.3	0.3	2.0	0.2
Traumatic brain injury	100.0	43.9	24.8	22.5	5.7	0.7	0.7	1.6	0.2
Developmental delay	100.0	61.6	20.8	16.2	0.7	0.1	0.5	0.2	#

#Rounds to zero.

[1] Other health impairments include having limited strength, vitality, or alertness due to chronic or acute health problems such as a heart condition, tuberculosis, rheumatic fever, nephritis, asthma, sickle cell anemia, hemophilia, epilepsy, lead poisoning, leukemia, or diabetes. [2] Data for 2006 and 2007 combine public and private schools and combine public and private residential facilities. [3] Students who are enrolled by their parents or guardians in regular private schools and have their basic education paid through private resources, but receive special education services at public expense. These students are not included under "Regular school, time outside general class" (columns 3 through 5). Note: Data are for the 50 United States, the District of Columbia, and the Bureau of Indian Education schools. Detail may not sum to totals because of rounding.

SOURCE: U.S. Department of Education, National Center for Education Statistics (2010. *The Digest of Education Statistics 2009* (NCES 2009-013), table 51. Accessed at http://nces.ed.gov/programs/digest/d09/tables/dt09_051.asp.

Category	Number (in thousands)	Percent
All children under 18	15, 451	20.7
White only, non-Hispanic	4, 850	11.9
Black	4,480	35.4
Hispanic	5,610	33.1
Asian	531	13.3

Table 5.2   Children Under 18 Living in Poverty, 2008

SOURCE: U.S. Bureau of the Census, *Income, Poverty, and Health Insurance Coverage in the United States: 2009*, Report P60, n. 238, Table B-2, pp. 62-7.

The question is simple—do you have what it takes to enter the classroom?

NOTES

1. "What Is National Board Certification?" http://www.nbpts.org/become_a_candidate/what_is_national_board_c

2. "Summary Health Statistics for U.S. Children: National Health Interview Survey," 2009, Appendix III, Table VI.

3. "Foster Care Statistics 2009," http://www.childwelfare.gov/pubs/factsheets/foster.cfm

4. http://www.nccp.org/profiles/index_32.html

5. http://www.usatoday.com/news/health/2008-11-02-kidsmedications_N.htm

6. http://www.cdc.gov/reproductivehealth/data_stats/index.htm

7. Centers for Disease Control, http://www.cdc.gov/teenpregnancy/AboutTeenPreg.htm

8. http://www.autism-society.org/about-autism/

9. http://www.cdc.gov/nchs/fastats/asthma.htm

10. http://www.cdc.gov/hiv/surveillance/resources/reports/2008report/

11. http://www3.law.ucla.edu/williamsinstitute/publications/FinalAdoptionReport.pdf

12. http://singleparents.about.com/b/2008/08/11/the-number-of-children-currently-living-with-a-single-parent.htm

13. http://www.time.com/time/nation/article/0,8599,1883966,00.html

14. http://pediatrics.about.com/od/childabuse/a/05_abuse_stats.htm

15. Ibid.

16. Ibid.

17. http://www.dosomething.org/project/mentor-children-incarcerated-parents

18. http://pediatrics.about.com/od/stds/a/309_std_stats.htm

19. http://www.troubledteens.com/information-and-statistics/troubled-teens-statistics-teen-help-for-troubled-teens.html

20. http://www.cdc.gov/Features/ChildrenAndSmoke/

II
WHAT TO EXPECT FROM CLASSROOM TEACHING

6

Salary

Let's get straight to the heart of the matter. Let's talk money. It's easy to find information about beginning teaching salaries state-by-state. Some examples are: Alaska ($24,100–$70,704); Michigan ($38,297–$71,046); Ohio ($24,051–$66,231); Texas ($40,800–$60,230); and Connecticut ($40,973–$90,998).[1]

This information is vital to have if you are interested in paying your bills. There are no bonuses for teachers, such as corporate people may receive. You can easily see the disparity in salaries from one state to another. School administrators make undisclosed salaries. Applications for administrators' positions generally list a range of money, but seldom give the exact amount. This is a point of contention for a lot of teachers.

Compare these figures to the recent (2011) salaries of the top career paths (from the National Association of College Employers):

"The average car payment is $378 over 63 months. Let's say that you invested $378 every month, instead of making car payments from age 30 to age 65 (35 years). If you average a rate of return of 12 percent, your money will grow to $2.4 million."[2]

The average rent/mortgage is about $900.00 (a very modest estimate). Do you see where this is going? Do the math. You may also have a student loan to repay. You may not be living as well as you think if you decide to dive into the world of teaching. Teaching will not make you well off. Remember, you still have to eat! By the time you pay taxes and pay for medical insurance, your beginner's take-home pay will be under $1,000.00 per paycheck. Be ready to live very frugally for a long while. Most districts max out your salary at year twenty-five. That means that after twenty-five years of service, you do not get any more raises.

Table 6.1 Salaries of the top career paths, 2011

Chemical engineer	$66,886
Computer science	$63,017
Mechanical engineer	$60,739
Electrical communications	$60,646
Computer engineer	$60,112
Systems engineer	$57,497
Engineer technology	$57,176
Information science and systems	$56,868
Business systems (networking/telecommunications)	$56,808

Source: National Association of College Employers (www.naceweb.org/home.aspx).

The salaries listed above for non-teaching jobs have teachers beat by a long shot. The "normal" increase per year is about 2–3 percent. This does not cover the rate of inflation or any life-changing occurrences, like getting married, having children, or supporting a family. Having an advanced degree gives you about $1,500.00 more per year than just having a college degree.

Most recently, there is a train of thought indicating that advanced degrees have no effect on student achievement. Very soon, there may not be programs in place that support tuition reimbursements.

Most states will have you pay into their retirement system, so you will not build up Social Security quarters. When you work outside of the school system (corporate jobs, blue collar, white collar), you build up Social Security quarters toward retirement. Not so as a teacher.

Your retirement deductions go into the state's pot of gold. These funds are held for you for the time when you retire from the system. Federal taxes are at the complete minimal level of deductions from your paycheck. If you stay in front of the problem, at tax time you can avoid paying a hefty tax bill.

Most district offices have appropriate forms to put additional deductions in place. You will need to figure out your tax bracket in order to deduct the necessary amount per check, so you don't to fall victim to the tax man. States do supply you with a teachers' retirement calculator. Most of these calculators can be found online.

You can determine your monthly worth before leaving the system. Just remember that every move can be costly. If you retire or resign early, you must pay an early withdrawal fee and pay taxes on the "income" you have received. Repeat: early withdrawal fees and taxes on income received. So, be sure this is something you want to do before withdrawing the money.

One option is to roll the money into an outside (private) retirement plan or build up a diversified stock portfolio. The take-home message is: Do something. Stay ahead of the money projections. Good budgeting techniques include having six months' worth of salary set aside for whatever comes.

Figure out a method of accomplishing this well in advance. Joining a savings club helps at holiday times. The money is removed before you get it, and it comes in handy at crucial times. Know this—your checks will barely make paying the bills. There won't be much left to save. Expect an exercise in futility. But do your best to stay in front of the problem. Arm yourself with loads of financial information.

There are alternative savings accounts in which you can deposit money for retirement. In some states, if you are married, you cannot receive your spouse's Social Security benefits when they retire. The states have total control over your money, your life insurance, your medical insurance, and your retirement funds.

During new-teacher orientation, ask questions. Know about your options and keep abreast of frequent changes. Because states allow school districts to govern their own regions, it is important to understand that when transferring from one state to another or from one district to another, you may lose benefits.

When you take into consideration the work teachers do to help advance society, you can easily wonder: "Why don't teachers make the kind of money that doctors do?" Here is a quote from a recent blog on teachers' pay:

> "In your comparison of teachers to lawyers and doctors, you left out that teachers have the easiest job, the least amount of required qualifications, the shortest education requirement and they only work three quarters of a year. People who sign up to be teachers have known their whole life that the teaching profession is not high paying. If they want more money, they should have pursued a different profession instead of putting children's education on the line while they extort the school district." (September 3, 2007)[3]

The point here is simple: *Perception*. The public perceives teachers as lofty creatures, not as professionals. Of course, professional people have offices. Don't they? Some people consider teachers as glorified babysitters.

In fairness to the people who train as doctors: Doctors spend at least eleven years (four years college/four years medical school/three years residency—at a minimum) in education and training after high school. They work twice as long as the average worker per week, and they work to repay student loans for about the first ten years after completing residency training. They arrive to the workplace "above the neck" in debt. Anyone can respect that.

Do you remember the days when teaching was considered a profession? There was a time when teaching meant that you were really smart, and smart was a valuable commodity.

There used to be a definite level of respect that was evident. A teacher could walk into any room and part the waters. At family gatherings, when the teacher would arrive, you could hear people leaning over to one another whispering, "She's a teacher."

Let's examine some things that teachers can do to correct and change the current perception.

For one thing, teachers are not required to undergo anything like the preparation required of doctors, in either the number of years required or the financial cost, which finds many new doctors burdened with a debt far beyond that experienced by any new teacher. The qualifications required to enter a medical training program exceed anything required by even the strictest teacher preparation program. It has been repeatedly noted that the standards to enter and successfully complete a teaching pre-service program at virtually any of the nation's 1,200 teacher education programs are the easiest of any collegiate professional degree program. The 1,200 teacher education programs not only vastly exceed the number of the nation's medical programs; they vary widely in their enrollments, with some so small that it is essentially impossible to have a quality program. Fewer than half of them, about 550, are accredited by NCATE, the National Council for the Accreditation of Teacher Education, and there are questions about the value of the NCATE accreditation program itself. Some of the nation's most respected schools of education, at prestigious institutions, don't bother to acquire NCATE (National Council for Accreditation of teacher Education) accreditation. Beyond the technicalities, however, there are other significant reasons why teachers aren't paid like doctors, and they never will be. One is the weight of numbers. There are five to six times as many public school teachers as there are doctors. Thus, even if in theory everyone agreed on equivalent pay, it would cost five to six times as much to pay teachers at the same average level as doctors. It will never happen. By and large, the public is not really concerned about the salaries of individual teachers, anymore than they are about the income of individual doctors. What they are concerned about is the total bill for public schooling; that is, the taxes they pay.[4]

It's all about taxes. The fallacy in this argument is that the public (in general) does not pay doctors via tax rolls. The fact in the argument is that teachers do get paid from taxes—in most cities. So, to raise teacher pay, taxes must increase.

Who's going to vote for higher taxes? See any hands? This is the main problem with public education. The money is tied to local, state, and, sometimes, federal money. Some states have tied teacher pay to gambling money. States say that their budgets are strapped. This may be true. Maybe teacher pay is tied to the wrong line item.

We can use a little innovation here. Maybe we can request that each family pay a very minimal fee per year for a child's education at a public school. This fee can offset costs incurred for academic activities, music and the arts, and additional resources for technology in the classroom.

In a small way, this very nominal fee ties parents to the school. Isn't that what we want to do? Right now, parents are absent. We need them to buy into their child's education. Public schools can charge nominal fees. And, there are ways that we can effectively utilize the resources that are already available. For now, the bottom line is: Don't expect to get rich from teaching.

Parents are absent.

The real challenge is getting our youth to *buy* into education. The school year could extend by one hundred more days and still not generate a return on the investment. So, an extended school year is not the answer. Before we have some knee-jerk reaction (again) to fix the educational system, let's take some time to reflect on phasing in common-sense strategies that we know can work.

Take the money out of the state's hands. Federal standards can help. Some may argue the political platforms regarding standardizing education. The United States currently ranks twenty-seventh in the world in education, at least in one area—science.

Drastic times call for drastic measures. As federal employees, the entire teaching structure would change. The burden would be relieved from the states' budgets. More money could be placed in the pockets of teachers and used for classroom resources. The insurance pool would be greater. Hence, insurance premiums would decrease and the take-home pay would increase.

This, in turn, would help feed more money into the economy. Millions of teachers fueling the economy would be a great thing. The economic impact of restructuring this giant would be tremendous. Of course, it would take a complete overhaul of our brains. We would probably have to be re-wired in order to survive.

The act of doing next to nothing or using polished methods with no substance will only set us back further than we are already.

A national policy would make it easier for school districts to maximize the performance of all teachers by offering teachers a standard base salary system. This policy has not yet been established.

Effective teachers could actually start circulating throughout the nation, and there would be no need for incentive pay for hiring teachers to work in urban areas or at high-risk schools. The changes that should be made need to happen quickly. The money (or lack thereof) is a real issue for American teachers.

Actually, a beginning teacher's salary, in some places, may be right above the poverty level. Teachers have resorted to food stamps. Could it be that not adequately paying our teachers is one of the ways in which the education system is failing our children?

NOTES

1. www.teachersalaryinfo.com
2. Damon Carr, "Automobiles Can Drive You Broke," November 8, 2005, http://www.finalcall.com/artman/publish/article_2267.shtml
3. Education Week Teacher, blog. http://blogs.edweek.org/teachers/webwatch/2008/04/an_epidemic_of_student_violenc.html.
4. David Kirkpatrick, Alexis de Tocqueville Institution, May 3, 2001, www.adti.net

7
Taxes

In this section, you will find a brief synopsis of how your personal money plays a part in your teaching career. You can claim school supplies as a tax deduction. Watch your federal deductions per pay period. If you are not paying enough federal (and, in some cases, state) taxes, you may be looking at a hefty tax bill.

Unless you resign, you cannot access your retirement fund. Keep all of your retirement reports in a special place. These reports are official documents. If the retirement fund is drawn down before a certain period, you may wind up paying a stiff penalty. Calculate the end result before making any hasty moves.

You do not receive Social Security benefits as a teacher unless you have worked in another profession that allows you Social Security benefits. Check your state's policies on these money matters.

If you are in another profession, think about this before changing careers to becoming a teacher. What would be the trade-offs if you decide to switch careers? Will you be better off staying at your current job? These are questions you must answer.

You can opt into the tax-sheltered program for childcare. If you choose to do this, you should pay attention to the rules governing childcare claims on your federal taxes. Everybody has different tax scenarios. The best advice is to seek out a tax expert to fit your particular needs. Some of the groundwork has been laid here. So you should have a good head start.

8

Your Student Loan

Face it—you are going to be in debt for a while if you have a student loan from college. The lifetime of your student loan could last past ten years. These loans contribute to the national debt. United States students are $535 trillion in debt.[1]

There are loan forgiveness programs and consolidation programs. Individual states do offer loan forgiveness programs. You will have to meet some criteria: work in an underrepresented academic area (i.e., science, math), teach disadvantaged students, and have proof of work for a certain amount of time at one school. Have a Plan B in effect while you work toward meeting these criteria. Some loan payments may be in the range of $200–$500 per month. You can work out your budget with a variety of financial software programs.

Currently, loan forgiveness programs are suffering due to the recession. So the burden will rest on your shoulders to take care of your obligation. The government and other lending institutions will see to it that their money is returned. If you default on the loan, the credit reporting agencies are notified, and your credit score will be severely affected. Your income can legally be garnished to repay the loan.

There are some school districts that reimburse you for classes taken toward advanced degrees. Remember, your salary will only increase about $1,500 per year with an advanced degree. Having a master's degree or doctorate always makes you more marketable.

Be aware. Be prepared.

NOTE

1. National Loan Debt Clock, 2008. http://www.finaid.org/loans/studentloandebtclock.phtml

9
Gossip

The truth about schools is that gossip exists everywhere, from the top to the bottom. Stay away from gossip. The teachers' lounge can be one of the havens for cliques. In every school, there are groups of teachers that other teachers refer to as "suck ups." These teachers are generally consulted by administrators and are allowed to get away with certain things that other people are held accountable for.

Every school has this group. This type of atmosphere builds division. This type of atmosphere fosters underachievers and hikes in attrition rates. Administrators will deny that this is the case—for job preservation reasons. But, the truth is in the statistics.

The statistics that describe violence in schools, low test scores, and teacher success all revolve around a core central element—incompetence in the classroom.

There is a direct correlation between the cliques that form and the ills that infiltrate the building. Some administrators come in with their own agendas. It's important for school districts to take a close look at the kind of people in charge of our children.

There is a line of thinking in the education community—and it is growing stronger—that school administrators should be obsolete. Teachers look to strong leaders for guidance. The goal should be closing achievement gaps.

Instead, the real challenge is the struggle between teachers and the powers that be. These statements are by no means an indictment of all administrators. However, good leaders often play second fiddle to the problems that plague the school systems. Too often, good administrators get worn down too soon.

The trickle-down effect, of course, is that children suffer.

Gossip, or any form of corruptive behavior, has no place in a productive culture. Ideally, we know what we have to do. We know what should be expected from good teachers. But we have to deal with the reality that it is present.

Very often, we pick up the local newspapers to find that a teacher may have been arrested for doing something illegal at a school, like having an inappropriate relationship with a student. How do you work with the whole without really becoming a part of it? Once again, use your best judgment.

It's not the best idea to hastily run out telling everybody in your department or on your team all of what you are going through in your personal life. In fact, the workplace is not the setting to discuss anything about your personal life at all. Teachers are in the business of teaching children.

Personal financial information or that you're getting a divorce are not topics of conversations for the workplace environment. In-person communication may set off some sparks, but the world of the Internet has opened up new and more adventurous avenues of communication.

You can be assured that the minute something happens, teachers and students will have e-mails, tweets, and Facebook posts going. There is no more mystery involved. So do your best to stay away from commenting about other people. These comments will get back. Your job may be jeopardized over gossip.

Stay away from discussing confidential information about students with other teachers or offering your personal opinion about the student. This is illegal. If a parent found out that his child was being discussed (especially in writing), that could be grounds for a major lawsuit. And these days, people are waiting around like vultures to file lawsuits.

So err on the side of caution. Be careful what you say out loud about a child. In sending text messages and e-mails to your colleagues, never use the name of a student. You can easily identify a student by her ID number or some other generic means.

Never send personal e-mails or text messages to students. This has become a serious issue. The students are considered minors. You will find that most districts have strict policies governing communications with students.

Teachers can be placed on "official notice" for violations regarding Facebook postings. If the violations are serious, a teacher can be dismissed immediately. Some states may even revoke your license, depending on the nature of the inappropriate behavior. Stay away from social networks that portray you as anything less than professional.

Children know how to obtain your information. Take care to protect yourself. Don't hang out your dirty laundry where children can possibly see it.

Please do not get sexually involved with anyone on the job or with a student. This is a certain last nail in the coffin. Over two thousand teachers were found guilty of having sexual relations with their students from 2002 to 2007.[1] In 2010, twenty-seven teachers lost certificates in Tennessee due to inappropriate touching, inappropriate contact with students, and sexual battery. A teacher was found to have shared a nude picture of himself in a text message with a student.

If you are found guilty of any of these crimes, you will serve jail time and have to register as a sex offender. Along with this, you will not be allowed to work with children again.

Each state has its own student-teacher contact policy. Stay *far* away from sexual relationships—with other adult colleagues and most specifically with any child. The latter could result in prison time. Also, don't forget about the age of technology.

Cell phones can record. Your situation will be on the Internet faster than you can blink your eyes. All of your hard work will be for nothing and on top of everything else you will be fired.

The best line of defense is to be exceptionally good at what you do. Separate your job from personal matters.

NOTE

1. Dorothy Neddermeyer, "Teacher Sexual Abuse of Students Increasing," November 5, 2007. http://www.selfgrowth.com/experts/dorothy_neddermeyer.html

10

Keeping Fit

Teaching is a job that requires you to be mentally and physically fit. Your body will feel tired most of the time. Make sure that you are eating properly and drinking lots of water. That brings me to the bathroom rule.

Teachers cannot leave their classes unattended. According to the National Educators Association, teachers rank high on bladder problems, along with nurses and pilots.[1] Think about this when you hear a teacher tell a student to "hold it." Ridding the body of urine can fight off infections.

It's important to keep fit, because teachers are in the business of teaching and modeling for students. Students translate how you look into how you care about yourself. One teacher was chosen every year by the graduating class at his school as Teacher of the Year. One of the students explained why this particular teacher was chosen consistently. He addressed us by saying: "Mr. Jones [not real name] is not only the best teacher at the school. He has to be the best dressed person I have seen in my life." There was a time when suits were the norm. Today, teachers come to school in T-shirts. If you think that how you present yourself to the students does not matter, think again.

Children are paying attention. The entire staff should be professionally dressed at all times, from head to toe. Any state or local official should be able to walk into a school and distinguish the faculty from the students.

Teachers should never dress like they are going to a barbeque. We can do much better than that. You don't have to have a lot of money to look fabulous. The outward appearance sets the inner mood. If you look good, you feel good. Start each day like this, and you will find teaching a pleasurable experience.

NOTE

1. *National Educators Association Today,* November 2004. http://neatoday.org

11

Illness

Teachers have higher rates of respiratory infections, chronic voice disorders, and musculoskeletal problems than people in other professions. Basically, we take care of other people before we care about ourselves.[1]

Most school schedules do not allow you adequate time to breathe. You will have about fifteen minutes to eat lunch. Yes, the schedule says thirty minutes. By the time the children exit the classroom and you get your things together, about ten minutes have slipped away. If you have to get in the cafeteria line, forget eating all together! Bring your lunch as much as possible. It saves time. You will have more time to sit, relax, and allow your food to digest. It's not healthy to eat too fast.

Become a well-oiled machine and develop a routine. Use this small amount of time to wind down. A school environment is not like the Google workplace, where everyone has ample opportunity to exercise, use flexible hours, and work at their own pace. Think about the impact that would have on schools.

Children just may start wanting to come to school! As much as the old school works, we can still incorporate that into a system that can accommodate the needs of the students. For instance: In a self-motivated structure, a student would come into a classroom, be ready to engage himself in the discussion, produce completed homework, and take tests on designated days.

The student would have weekly computer-generated progress reports, sign in and out at a terminal (at the door), take comprehensive exams, and have to give an oral presentation before graduating. Of course, this method would be diluted for primary grades. The teacher would act as the facilitator.

Innovation is what we need. Students and parents would know from the onset what is expected and what is required before moving to the next level. This method encourages total engagement from all stakeholders.

Exercise spaces can be a part of the day's activities. Some sort of physical activity should be required at least thirty minutes every day. Children could choose. At any one time, there might be dance classes, soccer classes, polo classes, horseback riding, tennis classes, golf classes, and so forth. A student would have to stick with his choice for four weeks. His grade would depend on his performance and knowledge of the rules of the game. All testing would be online.

This variety would give students more exposure, more marketability, and better physical fitness. We have locked children into a mold that most children don't fit. There is more obesity in young children today than at any time in the history of public schools. If we know more now about the science of food, then why are we having this problem?

Food waste is a huge problem. Scientists are studying "food behavior."[2] According to the Department of Agriculture, food waste is difficult to track. But, cafeteria workers know all too well how much food students throw away on a daily basis.

This food, a great deal unopened, cannot be donated. The food safety law prohibits that practice. As students move through the line, they are told that they have to choose from a variety of foods on the list of healthy items for the day. When eating is supposed to be a relaxing time, students are pressed to eat what they don't like and are given a short time in which to eat it.

Students get failing grades in physical education because they don't want to dress out. This is sending a huge message. They are ashamed of their bodies. Some can hardly fit into the gym uniform. It's unfortunate that there are no alternatives in which to engage our children.

One size does not fit all. I challenge schools to become more proactive in their attempts to overcome stigmas and to introduce a more welcoming physical fitness program for our children. You have read some suggestions here. They are only a start. With proper planning, a program like this can be extremely successful at your school.

In most school districts, you will get ten days per year for personal leave. Outside of that, your paycheck will experience a drop. Be prepared. You might want to pay for short-term and long-term disability. And did you know that maternity leave is considered an "illness"? The father cannot take maternity leave in some states. So, if your spouse is also a teacher, he would have to take his personal days as well. This would be more impact on your budget. Health insurance premiums will definitely eat into your paycheck.

Are you prepared to pay for a serious illness?

Teachers are more absent than students.[3] Teachers contract influenza viruses too frequently because parents send children to school sick. Parents cannot skip work. So who carries the load? Teachers do. By the way, put some money aside for anti-bacterial soap, germ-killing products, and loads of bleach. You will need to wipe down your desks, benches, and other work areas.

Here are some headlines and excerpts from real stories that you may find interesting.[4]

> "I retired from secondary teaching after only a year, due to a concern for my future mental health."

> "My first year of teaching was my last for a very long time. I was 24 and teaching emotionally disturbed high school students in a rural district. When I did go back (ten years later), I taught in elementary school, and I have been there ever since. I transitioned from teaching resource room, to an integrated spec ed and reg ed room, to a regular classroom. Most of my problems in my first year were due to inexperience, but I have to say that I wasn't supported in any way by the rest of the staff and the principal.
>
> In later years, I became a negotiator for our local union. It was in this role that I got acquainted with the discipline policy, or lack thereof, in supporting teachers who were being emotionally abused by parents and students, and sometimes other staff members. The district was very reluctant to put anything into our teacher contract that helped us. They would say that we were covered under the law. But, how easy is it for teachers to get a lawyer? Contracts are supposed to have language for the working conditions under which teachers work."

Nearly half of teachers have suffered from mental illness

It is interesting that a journal publication from 1978—"Mental Illness in School Teachers," from the *British Medical Journal*—still holds its own in these current times.[5] In the first paragraph, the entire consideration of what some teachers deal with is summarized very succinctly. H. MacAnespie writes:

> At a time when the medical profession is at last taking a serious view of mentally ill doctors, the problem of the mentally ill school teacher should be given more attention than it has received. Some teachers have continued to teach, perhaps for years, while suffering from manifest psychotic or psychoneurotic illness. Thus pupils may be exposed to the prolonged influence of a teacher with one or more serious psychiatric disturbances, such as thought disorder, paranoia, hallucinations, disorientation, aggressiveness, failure to relate to colleagues, and extreme unreliability; who may be unable to control the class, use vicious physical punishment, talk incessantly and inconsequentially; have poor standards of dress and personal habits, or be frequently late and absent.

Out of the 36 teachers surveyed, some admitted to having mental disorders, some exhibited "abnormal" behavior, and some had a history of seeing a psychiatrist. Out of this group, eleven were found to be schizophrenic.

Some may argue that this focus group was a small and restricted group. However, we must take into consideration that groups like this do exist. They may be diluted across the spectrum, but the study gives a pause for concern. Teachers do not come with medical records displayed—only teaching certificates and college degrees.[6]

Mental health of teachers does matter. As stated earlier, the students suffer while "outside" problems are studied and statistics are disaggregated for conclusions. This researcher concluded:

> Health examinations for entry into the teaching profession are managed quite differently from those for most other salaried professions. They are carried out at teacher training colleges; and no medical examination, apart from a chest x-ray film, is carried out by the employing authority before a teacher takes up his or her post. Yet some teachers who break down give a history of psychiatric episodes during student days. Some teachers, moreover, are basically unsuitable for the job, with possibly inadequate or vulnerable personalities, who have drifted into teaching without proper motivation; and these may also be at risk of breakdown. A teacher with a chronic disorder applying for a post can negotiate an interview successfully and take up the job before his personal difficulties come to light, and in this way can move round the country from one post to another. This danger could be obviated if the interviews were more searching, if references were always asked for and taken up, or if each authority provided screening medical examinations or an advisory service. A surprising amount of disruption may occur in a school before action is taken over a mentally ill teacher.[7]

One positive diagnosis in any of these categories could present enormous challenges for a classroom environment and the instruction of children.

It is no secret that the job of a teacher is extremely demanding. The current method of forceful training has given us teachers who are virtually impotent, as well as incompetent, at their jobs. It could be that the stress from these duties helps to uncover underlying problems that were present all along.

When anyone applies for a teaching position, he should be required to take and pass a psychological profile. School district officials should know exactly who they have in front of children. Training institutions should make it a requirement for teacher candidates. The demand for good teachers is at an all-time high.

The students are not the only ones being test-driven. Teacher candidates are as well. It would serve us well to pause to examine trainees not only for their academic aptitude, but for their mental soundness. School safety is the number one priority.

If there are teachers in our midst who have mental health issues, then this is an area that must be dealt with openly and honestly. First, these people need counseling. Second, they may need to be removed from the classroom until a diagnosis is made regarding their ability to manage a classroom. For years, we have been struggling to nail the one issue plaguing our schools.

Millions of dollars are currently being spent on getting more resources in the hands of our children, when it could merely take a simple test to determine if we are hiring competent people for the job. The job of teaching is stressful, despite the time off.

Too often, we sweep the root causes of problems under the rug instead of dealing with them head on. Hopefully, we will start immediately taking a closer look at the mental health of persons inside of the classroom and take the emphasis away from certification tests.

Below are some excerpts that you may find interesting:

Research by the Association of Teachers and Lecturers on three hundred secondary school teachers showed that abuse at the hands of pupils had left 46 percent taking antidepressants or facing long lay-offs from school because of stress.

The survey also revealed that 72 percent of teachers had considered quitting their jobs because they were worn out by some pupils' persistent disruptive behavior, such as threats, swearing, locking teachers out of classrooms, vandalizing school property, letting down car tires, stealing keys, throwing eggs at staff, and spitting at them. One in seven (14 percent) said they had suffered actually bodily harm from pupils.

"Student held in Tyler teacher's stabbing had long history of mental illness"
Lee Hancock, *The Dallas Morning News*, October 18, 2009

> We're putting people in a position where they aren't equipped.

"Stressed teachers suffer breakdowns: Teaching is the most stressful job in the UK and mental illness is on the rise, says the National Union of Teachers"
Polly Curtis, guardian.co.uk, April 13, 2009

"One study by the Health and Safety Executive . . . concluded that teaching is the most stressful occupation in the U.K. with 41.5% of teachers reporting themselves as 'highly stressed.'"

"The rate of suicide per 100,000 teachers in England and Wales is 14.20 compared with 10.25 per 100,000 people in the general population."

"Education Department Issues Sexual Violence Guidelines"
Jason Koebler, *U.S. News & World Report*, April 6, 2011

"The Department of Education issued guidelines Monday that will help school administrators and teachers deal with cases of sexual violence in the classroom.

In public high schools, there were 800 reported rapes or attempted rapes during the 2007–2008 school year, the most recent year for which data is available. There were an additional 3,800 reported incidents of sexual battery, according to the department."

"Climate of Violence Stifles City Schools: Efforts by Phila. administrators to stem the complex problem have fallen short"
John Sullivan, Susan Snyder, Kristen A. Graham, and Dylan Purcell, *The Philadelphia Inquirer*, March 27, 2011

"Hard lessons in the real problems of dealing with Britain's unruliest pupils"
Sarah Freeman, *The Yorkshire Post*, April 8, 2011

What does a violent student "look" like?

General Characteristics:

- Has a history of tantrums and uncontrollable angry outbursts.
- Characteristically resorts to name calling, cursing, or abusive language.
- Habitually makes violent threats when angry.
- Has previously brought a weapon to school.
- Has a background of serious disciplinary problems at school and in the community.
- Has a background of drug, alcohol, or other substance abuse or dependency.
- Is on the fringe of his/her peer group with few or no close friends.
- Is preoccupied with weapons, explosives, or other incendiary devices.
- Has previously been truant, suspended, or expelled from school.
- Displays cruelty to animals.
- Has little or no supervision and support from parents or a caring adult.
- Has witnessed or been a victim of abuse or neglect in the home.
- Has been bullied and/or bullies or intimidates peers or younger children.
- Tends to blame others for difficulties and problems s/he causes her/himself.
- Consistently prefers TV shows, movies, or music expressing violent themes and acts.
- Prefers reading materials dealing with violent themes, rituals, and abuse.
- Reflects anger, frustration, and the dark side of life in school essays or writing projects.
- Is involved with a gang or an antisocial group on the fringe of peer acceptance.
- Is often depressed and/or has significant mood swings.
- Has threatened or attempted suicide.
- May be very unassuming and unsuspicious.

(List taken from the School Safety Handbook)

The Family Educational Rights and Privacy Act (FERPA) (20 U.S.C. § 1232g; 34 CFR Part 99) is a federal law that protects the privacy of student education records.[8] States have flexibility in disclosing information regarding students' records.

There have been numerous court cases filed for the sole purpose of obtaining information regarding a student's background, especially when the student comes into a classroom directly from juvenile centers or some other part of the criminal justice system. Of course, on the surface, it seems as though any teacher would have the right to know. Schools are supposed to be safe places to work and to learn.

According to many of the court decisions, teachers get whatever information the school administration deems necessary, along with probation officers. Most of the time, a teacher struggles in the classroom with these students. The primary focal point is reaching the child. That task becomes difficult when the teacher does not have firm knowledge of how best to convey the message.

Oftentimes, a great deal of class time is spent to discipline the child. These kinds of students have a greater tendency to disrupt the learning environment. This kind of environment may also promote bullying and adverse peer pressure. The law supersedes whatever we may think should happen.

As you know, knowledge is power. So know that you might have a variety of issues in the room and might not be equipped with sufficient information to thoroughly teach these children. The teacher argument also relies on the fact that teachers feel uncomfortable. This makes for a poor learning structure.

No teacher will be able to give it her all if she is constantly watching her purse or overly concerned about the safety of the other students. Teachers sometimes contend that the court system has no idea what really goes on inside of the capsule of the classroom. If the judges were more in touch, they might think again about the decisions they hand down regarding difficult-to-manage children in the classroom.

The notion of free and equal education comes into play again. How can any child receive equal instruction if the teacher is consumed with controlling one student or a few students? It is humanly impossible.

NOTES

1. Directors of Health Promotion and Education.
2. http://www.ers.usda.gov/Briefing/FoodNutritionAssistance/funding/behaveconawards.htm
3. *Journal of General Psychology* 155 (1994): 409–21.
4. http://www.teach-the-brain.org/forums/archive/index.php/t-47.html
5. *British Medical Journal* 2 (1978): 257–58.
6. www.ncbi.nlm.nih.gov/pmc/articles/PMC1606311/pdf/brmedj00136-0033.pdf
7. Ibid.
8. http://www2.ed.gov/policy/gen/guid/fpco/ferpa/index.html

12

It's Lunch Time

It's lunchtime. You will have to suck your food down like a vacuum cleaner. Don't ever count on the full thirty minutes. Who came up with thirty minutes anyway? Somewhere between the variety of union negotiations and traditional school days, the idea regarding thirty minutes stands firm.

The law states that students cannot be left unsupervised. So be aware that bathroom breaks are at a premium. Some of your lunchtime will be spent going to the restroom. Most schools have a duty-free lunchtime because of labor laws. Any worker should be given at least a half-hour to eat. That is pretty standard.

Should you eat in the school cafeteria? That is a good question. The subject of school lunch is another book all by itself. Let's ask the basic questions: Can you afford the lunch? Will you have time to get lunch, given the limited amount of time to eat? Is your money worth the portions you receive? Can you sue if you get food poisoning?

The most important component is the consideration of time. Is your classroom close enough to the cafeteria where you can retrieve a lunch, stand in line (you can jump ahead on occasion), and pay for the meal? Is the food worth the money? Can you sue the school? More than likely, the answer would be "no." It would be difficult to prove the origin of the food ailment if there are not several other people showing symptoms.

Your best bet is to make yourself content. Sit with another teacher or by yourself inside your classroom. Relax. The bell will be ringing soon.

The traditional school day and lunch program have come under a great deal of scrutiny in the past decade. Our schedule still reflects a time when children came to school while the parents took care of the farm. How many children fit this description today?

The school calendar, lunchtime, class periods, vacation time, and other holidays are a product of—well, a long time ago. The calendar doesn't look like it will be changing anytime soon, because our school day helps parents who work that 9–5 job. The parent is serviced from beginning to end. Our school calendar also fits the "normal" vacation time for the summer.

The amount of time that teachers and students have to eat is not long enough. If you work at a school where more than three hundred students have to go through the line, you must wonder how much time the last child in line has to eat. So what if a child doesn't get to eat?

There is no variety and healthy food is not part of the menu. The food is lifeless at most schools. The students hang out in the yard during lunchtime. Some kids bring their lunch, but not many. Bringing your lunch is viewed as embarrassing. It is surprising that students are turned away at the cashier if they are not current on their account.

There are horror stories of administrators running after students to throw their meals away if the students' accounts are negative. As a teacher, you will have to observe what's going on with your students. If you happen to see a child wandering around directly after the lunch bell, he probably doesn't have any money.

There are children on free and reduced lunch. With all the help that the kids may be privileged to, they still find a way to degrade another child who is getting free lunch. There have been cases where $0.40 was enough to turn away a student from eating.

Where is this entire thing going? How can you teach a hungry child? You cannot. Also, check the rules. You may not be allowed to feed students. A new focus on obesity encouraged legislators to look at how bringing outside food to school for children affects their health—never mind the fact that school lunch is delivered frozen, pre-packaged, and ready to be heated.

Ann Cooper, the "renegade lunch lady," is doing a great job at launching a school lunch initiative for children to eat healthier food. The obesity matter is no accident. Most school lunch food contains too much fat and preservatives. She helps the kids grow vegetables and fruit in a school garden. The children take care of a garden and pick the food when ripe. The food is then transferred to the cafeteria for cleaning and/or cooking. The children are eating homegrown food and learning an invaluable lesson on how to eat healthier meals. This is what is referred to as a lifelong lesson. Also, the First Lady of the United States, Michelle Obama, has taken on a national initiative to increase awareness of childhood obesity.

Think about the money school districts could save by growing their own fruits and vegetables. The irony is—we established the school schedule around farming and we forgot about farming!

Food is extremely important. Most scientists will tell you that it's not healthy to rush eating your food. Partially chewed food takes longer to digest and makes the body's digestive system work harder. The first site of digestion is inside of the mouth. Eating should take place under relaxed conditions. Lunchtime is anything but relaxed.

We just do what we're told.

13

The Players' Network

Talk to any veteran teacher, and she or he will assure you that if you stick around long enough, someone is going to hit on you, married or not. Be advised: Stay away from trouble. If your gut instincts detect something unusual, listen. Sexual predators lurk in all areas of society, but what better microcosm than a school environment? Sure beats the grocery store meetings.

It's never a good idea to date someone you work with. The word gets around fast. Sometimes, even the students know. So prepare yourself for rumors. You will be tested.

A school is a place where life happens. This is a unique job. You will get to see people come and go, babies born (not literally), people get ill, and people who will die.

Dating someone on the job only complicates the issue. The students talk to each other. They bring it home to the parents. The community knows about the "goings-on." The students will also talk about your business to the other teachers. The snowball continues to roll. Always protect your reputation and guard your actions.

The rules for good conduct on any professional job hold true for classroom teachers. There is a standard of conduct that all teachers should uphold. Of course, in reality, we realize that not everyone will follow the rules. But if enough people do, the likelihood of running a well-oiled machine is greater.

The goal is to model a role that we want our children to imitate.

Additionally, you can be immediately fired for inappropriate sexual activity at a school. It's not worth the drama.

14

Know Your Rights

What if . . .? Know your rights. Read the handbook, for God's sake. Read your contract. Don't just sign it. You may see a clause towards the end that states that you have to "perform any assigned duties." School districts pay attorneys a lot of money to keep them out of trouble. So how can you protect yourself?

You will definitely need to join a teachers' organization that provides you with legal assistance and lawsuit coverage. If you can spare the time, read a legal book written to explain the law behind some of the rules and regulations at your school. It is also a good idea to subscribe to a legal Web site for your state.

Keep up with cases involving school-related challenges. You may be surprised at the types of rulings that take place on a daily basis.

Be sensible. People love to sue. As a teacher, you have no extra money to give to anyone for any reason. Ask questions of your representing group, and get involved in the decision-making processes. Again, it is wise to read the papers you sign and to ask questions.

At times, contracts can be written in complicated language, which discourages average people from taking the time to read the actual document. It may call for taking the contract home, examining the language, and signing it after all the bases have been covered. If there is something that makes you feel uncomfortable, then do not sign it.

Employers count on employees not reading the contract to its fullest. Teachers, especially, must stay on top of changing legal language. In this climate, this is vital to surviving the market.

15

Using the School Computer

There are laws that protect children from having free reign of the Internet at school. According to the Federal Communications Commission (FCC):

> The Children's Internet Protection Act (CIPA) is a federal law enacted by Congress to address concerns about access to offensive content over the Internet on school and library computers. CIPA imposes certain types of requirements on any school or library that receives funding for Internet access or internal connections from the E-rate program—a program that makes certain communications technology more affordable for eligible schools and libraries.

- Schools and libraries subject to CIPA may not receive the discounts offered by the E-rate program unless they certify that they have an Internet safety policy that includes technology protection measures. The protection measures must block or filter Internet access to pictures that are: (a) obscene, (b) child pornography, or (c) harmful to minors (for computers that are accessed by minors). Before adopting this Internet safety policy, schools and libraries must provide reasonable notice and hold at least one public hearing or meeting to address the proposal.
- Schools subject to CIPA are required to adopt and enforce a policy to monitor online activities of minors.
- Schools and libraries subject to CIPA are required to adopt and implement an Internet safety policy addressing: (a) access by minors to inappropriate matter on the Internet; (b) the safety and security of minors when using electronic mail, chat rooms, and other forms of direct electronic communications; (c) unauthorized access, including so-called

"hacking," and other unlawful activities by minors online; (d) unauthorized disclosure, use, and dissemination of personal information regarding minors; and (e) measures restricting minors' access to materials harmful to them.

Schools and libraries are required to certify that they have their safety policies and technology in place before receiving E-rate funding.

- CIPA does not affect E-rate funding for schools and libraries receiving discounts only for telecommunications, such as telephone service.
- An authorized person may disable the blocking or filtering measure during any use by an adult to enable access for bona fide research or other lawful purposes.
- CIPA does not require the tracking of Internet use by minors or adults.

Most school computers contain filtering software that detects keystrokes or built-in Web site information that prevents students from sexting or transferring inappropriate images from one computer to the next. For teachers, using a school computer for accessing personal e-mails can prove to be risky business.

The best practice in this regard is to wait to read personal e-mails, do personal banking, or take care of any other personal business at home. School technology personnel can obtain your e-mails, passwords, and credit card information. There is hardly anything that you can do to prevent the school technology staff from viewing what you look at on a school computer.

Some wireless access devices can also pick up when you are using your cell phone to text or access the Internet while at school. Take the advice and stay clear of the social networking sites while you are at school. It is important to know the reality of the situation. Your "friendly" networking can backfire on you. For example, a Dallas, Texas, student manipulated a picture of her principal on her Facebook page and wrote that the principal was a lesbian. Since then, you may notice that administrators in quite a few places have taken their pictures off the school's home page. Oddly enough, teachers are not using computer-based instruction as much as they should.

Below are some headlines that you may find interesting:

- "Florida High School Teacher Fired Over Internet Pictures and Part-Time Work," Jonathan Turley, May 4, 2008[1]
- "Teacher Fired over MySpace Photo," Greg Franzese, January 21, 2008[2]
- "Transgendered teacher fired after announcing gender reassignment treatment," Brian Norris, October 15, 2009[3]
- "Morristown teacher fired after sending text messages to student," Sharon Adarlo, *The Star-Ledger*, August 22, 2009[4]

- "Facebook and teachers: Still a potentially dangerous combination for your career," Maureen Downey, *The Atlanta Journal-Constitution*, August 23, 2010[5]
- "Teachers Fired for Flirting on Facebook with Students," by Perry Chiaramonte and Yoav Gonen, *The New York Post*, October 18, 2010[6]
- "Teachers Fired for Social Media Photos—Morality, Fitness for Duty, or Lack of Judgment?" Teresa Thompson, May 9, 2011[7]
- "Teachers, students and Facebook, a toxic mix," Bob Sullivan, October 22, 2010[8]

If teachers can keep in mind that any classroom action could have legal consequences, it makes a difference in how behaviors occur. Additionally, these "consciousness" keeps teachers within the boundaries of good instruction instead of injecting personal attitudes toward a particular topic. The best medicine for this problem is to be proactive. The worse scenario is reaction. If a student asks you to be his "friend" on Facebook, the answer is always "No."

It might also be wise to guard against taking on friends who are colleagues. It is hard to control who connects with whom. Once the information is out and connections are made, the associations are cemented.

A judge can subpoena this information if required. Students can use Facebook to ruin your career.

Use common sense!

NOTES

1. http://jonathanturley.org/2008/05/04/florida-high-school-teacher-fired-over-internet-pictures-and-part-time-work/
2. http://www.reputationdefenderblog.com/2008/01/21/teacher-fired-over-myspace-photo/
3. http://blog.toronto-employmentlawyer.com/transgendered-teacher-fired-after-announcing-gender-reassignment-treatment
4. http://www.nj.com/news/index.ssf/2009/08/morristown_teacher_fired_after.html
5. http://blogs.ajc.com/get-schooled-blog/2010/08/23/facebook-and-teachers-still-a-potentially-dangerous-combination-for-your-career/
6. http://www.foxnews.com/scitech/2010/10/18/teachers-fired-flirting-facebook-students/#ixzz1No1HazMO
7. http://www.networkedlawyers.com/teachers-fired-for-social-media-photos-%E2%80%93-morality-fitness-for-duty-or-lack-of-judgment/
8. http://redtape.msnbc.msn.com/_news/2010/10/22/6345537-teachers-students-and-facebook-a-toxic-mix

16

It's *Your* Attitude

Teachers set the example. Students emulate what they see. How a teacher maintains a routine, conducts business with other teachers or administrators, and physically presents herself provides an opportunity for students to see the value of learning. There are numerous books written on how to improve classroom instruction.

Succinctly speaking, you can become your own worst enemy. Tackling so many different personalities at one time can be rough. Take an honest inventory of your personal feelings and prejudices. Are you biased against people of color? Do you judge boys who wear their pants below their waists? Do you teach more to boys than to girls? Do you really care about your job?

Before you walk into that classroom, make sure that you know yourself and that you are comfortable with who you are. Be smart. Stay ahead of the game. Shake up your method from time to time. Stick with structure and mix up routine. Be a bit unpredictable. It's just like what law officers tell us about routinely walking the dog. Sometimes, it's a good idea to take a different route. In short, don't let them see you bothered about anything.

> Remember—she's somebody else's child.

Sleep deprivation affects your attitude. Think about ways in which you can relax. What are some activities that you enjoy? As a classroom teacher, you will not have the liberty of driving off to conduct business in the middle of the day without abiding by some regulations. If you are currently working in another profession, take inventory and compare the advantages to the disadvantages of what teaching has to offer. Is this what you really want to do? Will teaching be a drastic change for you? If so, you might not want to leave your present job. Just be honest with yourself.

Changing jobs can be painful; especially if it turns out that you're not happy with the end result.

So, much introspection is required before you take the giant plunge into the world of classroom teaching. Remember to know yourself. Go back to the section on mental health. Is there a history of mental health issues in your family? Have you had a psychological test? Have you visited a psychiatrist for a profile? Are you currently on medication for a mental health problem?

Teachers have to be aware that what they say and do is like gospel to the children. Children mimic teachers all the time. If you go back into your school history, the teacher who you recall the most is the one who made the greatest impact.

Conversely, you will also recall the one who did you the most wrong. That wrong sits with you for a long time. You can probably remember the event as if it had just occurred. That's why every little thing counts, and every second matters. Children don't miss you blinking your eye.

Conclusion:
The New American Classroom

"Always dream and shoot higher than you know you can do. Don't bother just to be better than your contemporaries or predecessors. Try to be better than yourself."

—William Faulkner

Today's classrooms are filled with challenges. These challenges are widely known and widely publicized. What is not widely known is that the solution is very simple. The real challenge is accepting the simple solution. Until we realize that students cannot learn unless we are honest with them, then any other method we design is just a waste of time. Money is not the answer to the problem. Money complicates the problem.

Disparity in educational funding is at the heart of many debates about how children learn. The information presented here only scratches the surface of recognizing what we face each day in this country regarding classroom teaching. The one true message that you should take away from all of this is that children do not respond well to liars.

We cannot continue teaching children empty courses that they know will not take them into the future. And, in this lies the problem. The educational structure should be updated immediately ("yesterday"). The old structure calls for a radical revival. Far too many children turn away from school while we waste time studying data and reporting statistics. The thousands of dropouts are quickly adding to the deficit and the lagging economy. Besides that, we are losing potential brainpower that could potentially solve global problems. And we cannot afford to lose.

With the current educational system, we lose young minds to the streets in numbers too high to contemplate. Since children are bored and uninterested, it is imperative that we change. Local governments and state governing bodies dictate traditional models.

Here we go—let's make that change!

Every classroom should be like a science classroom—built around inquiry-based learning. Every classroom should be equipped with at least four teachers. These teachers will act as a team. This group of individuals will cater to the particular needs of each student. Lessons are tailored to the academic level of each student. Each student is constantly engaged. There is 100% participation. The four teachers should hold degrees in a variety of areas; namely science, english, math, and history. Lessons are integrated to include all four areas with each assignment.

The team seeks out activities that incorporate global issues, promote original thinking, and encourage problem solving. The class can be divided into sections in which groups of students are working on a variety of assignments all at once. Students are mobile most of the time and have easy access to instructors.

This type of atmosphere promotes total peer inclusion in instruction. The team of teachers will become full-time facilitators, which is the wave of the future for teaching.

These teams can act as a model for students, in that problems are solved through cooperation instead of through individual work. The model shows students how to work together in a somewhat random yet organized environment.

The entire mode of instruction is immersed in technology. Students use computers for reading and research. They use a variety of software programs to create presentations, understand the principles of technology, and to design new programs.

Students get to observe their peers in action. While one group is working on a science procedure, another group is researching information for a group presentation. To accommodate this new model, the physical classroom would have to be bigger. Instead of the normal standard-sized room, the new classroom might take up an entire floor of a building. The old walls can be knocked down.

Students can interact with every aspect of their learning all of the time. They are free to have the time they need to discuss and debate issues with their peers, and to diplomatically argue through solutions.

This model presents a unique opportunity for teachers to actually teach. So many teachers would want a chance to work at one of these schools that there would be a line of applicants wrapped around the school. Teaching a child should not be considered a job. It is a passion.

The students will be encouraged to research topics for general discussion. Each student will prepare verbal assessments and with each delivery be responsible for understanding the connections between subjects.

Assessments should be authentic. Students are allowed the use of technology and would be required to formulate a plan of study of their own design. For children in earlier grades, parents will be asked to design a plan for their child.

Parents meet with teachers. Parents choose teachers they prefer for their child. Parents play a vital role in having a stake in the child's education.

The parents are required to spend a specified number of hours coming to school teaching the children a topic. All parents will be teaching at some time. Sound like chaos? Watch the results and report back later. If implemented correctly, students should have no time to waste.

The sooner students are engaged in this type of school, the more smooth the transition into adolescence and adulthood. And the child is more likely to discuss school-related activities at home with parents. For those children without parents or who have parents who have to work, the legal parent will assign a surrogate. Someone will represent each child, even if it is a big brother or big sister.

The idea is to get everyone involved with as little resistance as possible and to ensure the most success with the least amount of effort possible.

The success of the team approach depends on the strength of the team of teachers. Preferably, each team would be responsible for forming a group that promotes forward thinking. This would mean that either collectively or individually, the teams would have to publish papers or abstracts every year.

Staying sharp is the key to making this model work. The teacher teams would be sharp and on the cutting edge. Students would be able to see right away the contrast between what they used to learn in isolation and the new logic of learning concepts at a higher order of thinking. Appreciation of school will begin to set in. Once that happens, the students are hooked.

This method would raise test scores immediately. Classes should always remain open for visitors. The entire community can be engaged in how students learn. And, the community can come in to learn as well.

This method has so many advantages on which to build. It requires a new way of viewing how children are educated and what works best for children. It requires us to change our attitudes about teaching, what is required to become a certified teacher, and how to attract people who are called to teach, to include all children, and to accept their cultural differences.

A proposed new school mission:

> I (student) am not going to school. I am chasing my dream. This is not work for me. This is my passion. Passions have to be born, cultivated, and groomed. I intend to complete my goals, to return service to society, and to be a model for ethical behavior.

Out with the old	In with the new
One teacher per classroom	Team of teachers in one classroom
Discipline problems	100% engaged students
Isolated disciplines	Integrated curricula
Class-size challenges	Teams can manage more students
Traditional assessments	Authentic assessments
Memorizing facts	Original works including facts
Paper/pencil worksheets	Digital portfolios
Textbooks	Technology-based delivery
Order resources from companies	Build/design with material available from community
Traditional teacher evaluations	Collaboration/cooperation
Keep children at grade levels	Allow children to move on once mastering concepts
Individual assessments	Group portfolio
Community involvement at school meetings	Community engaged at school during school hours
Frozen cafeteria food	Food commissioned from local farmers
"Categories" of children (e.g., economically disadvantaged)	No labels for any child
Minimal extracurricular involvement	100% engagement
Moderately fair equal education	Removal of all biases
Centralized (local) education	Global connections
Substitutes for teacher absences	Reduced absences/no need for substitutes
Few to no fieldtrips	Activities external to the classroom part of curriculum
High attrition rate	Retention
Hours of school day	Tailored to the success of students

Table C.1

The new classroom of team teachers (teaching all subjects at one time) reaches children at their cognitive level without interruption. The student progresses when ready, rather than being held back according to rules regarding age. The age-based model suppresses genius and encourages frustration. In this new system, there is no room for traditional grading techniques.

Every child will have the accommodations necessary for complete success. True, each student moves at his own pace. And that fits into this model better than it does into the old paradigm.

Assessments take place at a more holistic level. Students would be required to maintain a portfolio for final assessment. This portfolio will act as the "communicator" during conferences, the "accountable evidence" for final grading, and the "document in focus" for class presentation.

Students get to witness teamwork in action. Good managerial skills involve knowing how to work with other people and how to construct models for ultimate cooperation. Among the reasons that some researchers cite for students having the wrong impression about scientific research are:

1. Students think they cannot be wrong.
2. They hardly ever see a team of people working together to solve a problem.
3. They feel like they have to find the answers alone.

This real-world experience shows them that they can work toward a common goal with other people. This model also teaches children how to trust other people, how to rely on strong positive individuals who do not mind coming to someone's aid.

This model encourages ethical behavior amongst the adults involved. In a way, it is a win-win solution for both teachers and students. It takes the burden from one teacher and spreads the responsibility to the group. No one teacher should have to cover up her limitations to the extent that it becomes burdensome.

This model is analogous to a relay race or a tag-team match in wrestling: "One for all and all for one." The success of the team depends on each person. This is the winning strategy.

The new model fosters a climate of easier access for parents and stakeholders. The school would be more accountable for quality results. Tutoring can take place inside of the classroom during school time instead of in after-school sessions. Some at-risk children may not be able to stay after school or attend special Saturday tutoring sessions. Sports must also be an integral part of this new model. This is yet another reason that those tutorial sessions should take place during school hours.

It is projected that within the next ten years, every person in the world will own an electronic device. That's a lot of electronic devices that we must acknowledge will have an impact on the approaches we use to effectively instruct children.

www.ingramcontent.com/pod-product-compliance
Lightning Source LLC
Chambersburg PA
CBHW031714230426
43668CB00006B/208